First Corinthians

Discovering God's Wisdom

"I rejoice in Your word like one who discovers a great treasure."
Psalm 119: 162

Linda Osborne

Unless otherwise noted, all Scripture quotations are from the NEW AMERICAN STANDARD BIBLE®, Copyright © 1960, 1962, 1963, 1968, 1971, 1972, 1973, 1975, 1977, 1995 by The Lockman Foundation. Used by permission.

Published by Catch the Vision! Press
909 E Palm Avenue, Redlands, CA 92374

ISBN-10: 1727738276
ISBN-13: 978-1727738278

CONTENTS

OTHER BOOKS/BIBLE STUDIES
BY THE AUTHOR

Called to Lead: Catch the Vision!
1 and 2 Timothy & Titus: The Final Letters
1 & 2 Thessalonians: He's Coming Soon!
Acts: Church Alive!
Colossians: Christ Supreme
David: Shepherd of Israel
Ephesians: Blessed!
Exodus: Deliverance
Galatians: Born (again!) to Be Free
Genesis: Beginnings
James: Let's Grow Up!
John: The Gospel of the Beloved
Philippians: Unrestrained Joy!
Revelation: Seven Letters to Seven Churches
Romans: The Gospel According to Paul
Ruth: A Love Story
The Women: Part One
The Women: Part Two
The Women: Part Three
The Women: Part Four
and
Lunch-Hour Lessons: Revelation

PREFACE

This year we are studying the epistle to the Corinthians written by the apostle Paul. "Epistle" is an important sounding word which simply means *letter*. Paul was writing a letter to his friends in Corinth. The year was approximately A.D. 55; Paul was on his 3rd missionary journey and was currently ministering in Ephesus. He had received some news that troubled him: news of division, sin, immorality, lawsuits between believers, marriage problems, difficulties, abuses, and disorderly conduct. Paul's letter was written in response to these problems.

Paul had established this church in Corinth only a few years earlier during his 2nd missionary journey. He stayed in Corinth for eighteen months, ministering first in the synagogue and then in the home of a Gentile. Paul loved these people and was concerned about their spiritual welfare. In his letter to them he addressed such doctrinal themes as the nature of the church, the nature of the believer's union with Christ, God's wisdom, proper worship, the Lord's Supper, spiritual gifts, and the resurrection of the dead; along with the practical themes of unity, church leadership, church discipline, lawsuits, marriage and divorce, Christian freedom and responsibility, worship, love, and ministry.

The foremost problem of the Corinthian church was that their focus was wrong. It was misplaced. That fact is seen in every problem they had, most significantly in their problem with unity. They were focusing on themselves, on other people, and on human wisdom rather than on Christ and the cross. How much of a difference would it make in *your* life if you learned this basic truth that the focal point of Christianity and the Christian life—therefore of the Christian himself—must be Christ and His cross, "For the message of the cross is … the power of God" (1 Corinthians 1:18), and that Christ is the key to every problem?

Our study is entitled, "Discovering God's Wisdom." Jesus Christ is the wisdom of God! Colossians 2:2-3 speaks of "God's mystery, that is Christ Himself, in whom are hidden all the treasures of wisdom and knowledge." We want to dig deep as we go about our study this year, seeking to unfold all that our Lord has to teach us of His wisdom through this very practical Christ-centered letter, written by the Holy Spirit for every believer today. Begin your year by asking God to reveal His Son to you through the power of His Holy Spirit and, throughout the year, to help you center your focus on *Jesus Christ and Him crucified!*

FIRST CORINTHIANS: *THE WISDOM OF GOD*
LESSON 1
1 CORINTHIANS 1

⚜

Day 1
Read 1 Corinthians 1:1-9

Note: The Sosthenes mentioned in verse 1 is probably the same one mentioned in Acts 18:17: the synagogue leader who seems to have been the head of the group opposing Paul. If he is the same one, then he eventually came to Christ!

1. Paul sets the stage for all that is to come in his letter by reminding the Corinthians *first* about whom they are and what they've been given:

   Whom they are: From verse 2 share what Paul tells them about themselves as Christians.

   ⚜

   ⚜

   ⚜

   What they've been given:

   ⚜ verse 4
   ⚜ verse 5
   ⚜ verse 7
   ⚜ verse 8

2. You may notice that the name of Jesus Christ is given or referred to in every verse in this passage. Paul's emphasis in these verses and throughout his writings comes in the small phrase "in Christ." Share what you think it means to be "in Christ" (verses 2 and 4). You may see John 15:5.

a. Do you know that you are "in Christ" today? You can *know* this! It is as simple as believing that Jesus Christ is the Son of God who died on the cross for *your* sins, and rose again on the third day (1 Corinthians 15:3-5). Because He died, your sins can be forgiven; because He lives, you can receive new life—*His life*! If you want this new life, read and follow Romans 10:8-10.

3. Ephesians 1:3-14 and 2 Peter 1:3-4 tell us about the blessings we have been given "in Christ." List as many as you can of these exciting truths:

Ephesians 1:3-14

2 Peter 1:3-4

In 1 Corinthians 1:9, Paul puts the emphasis where it belongs—not on the Corinthians themselves but on their God: *"God is faithful."*

4. If a church or a Christian is struggling, how would this fact make a difference in their thought process?

5. How might these things, of which Paul has reminded them in his opening thoughts, be the beginning of encouragement toward unity?

Making It Personal

6. Do you consider yourself a grateful person? Considering all that has been done for you "in Christ," what should be your attitude toward God and toward life?

Digging Deeper

✣ Corinth: Using the introduction to 1 Corinthians in your Bible or a Bible dictionary, share a little background on Corinth. You may also want to look for Corinth on your Bible map.

✣ Optional: Read 1 Corinthians in its entirety. You may also want to read Acts 18:1-18a, as it tells the story of Paul's experience in Corinth.

✣ Do your best to summarize today's passage in a couple of sentences.

Memory Verse

"For the word of the cross is to those who are perishing foolishness, but to us who are being saved it is the power of God." 1 Corinthians 1:18

Day 2
Read 1 Corinthians 1:10-17

In verse 10, Paul begins his exhortation to the church in Corinth. Actually, verse 10 is the key verse of the entire letter, in that it contains the first and foremost reason Paul wrote the letter—division in the church.

1. How was the division in this church manifested according to "Chloe's people"? (vv. 11-12)

   a. Describe what you think was actually happening here.

2. We might think that the "Christ party" ("I of Christ"), was the group that was on the right track. But Paul lists it along with the others making it appear that it too was a negative. What might the attitude of the "Christ party" have been?

3. To whom alone is the church to be loyal? How did Paul imply this in verse 13?

4. Why do you think Paul makes a point of saying that his preaching wasn't *in cleverness of speech?* (v. 17)

Making It Personal

5. What is Paul's exhortation to those who are causing division? v. 10

    a. Does this mean you can't think for yourself or have any differing points of view over non-doctrinal matters? What does it mean?

6. What can you do to help keep the unity in your home church? *(Are you doing anything that might bring disunity?)*

Digging Deeper

✤ Determine who each of these individuals were and why someone might have set their loyalty upon them:

Paul—1 Corinthians 1:1, Acts 18:1-8

Apollos—Acts 18:24-19:1a

Cephas—John 1:42

✣ Although this passage is speaking in particular of the divisions within a church body, this problem was a sign of things to come in the church as a whole. Should there be denominations in the church? Share your thoughts on why or why not.

✣ Do your best to summarize today's passage in a couple of sentences.

Day 3
Read 1 Corinthians 1:18-31

So far in his letter to his friends in Corinth, Paul has spoken to them about who they are, what they've been given in Christ, and the underlying cause of the problems in their church. In so doing, Paul points them to the only One to whom their loyalty belongs—Jesus Christ. Paul finishes by making the point that, although he was called to preach the gospel, even his preaching was not done in human cleverness or with worldly wisdom. All that he did and even the way he did it, was designed to keep the emphasis on the cross of Christ. The reason he did this follows in the profound portion of Scripture we will study today. It has been said that it would take a lifetime to unpack and apply all that is taught in these verses. We would do well to try!

1. Paul has just spoken of human cleverness (v. 17). Is the message of the cross "clever" to the unsaved? (v. 18) What is it?

   a. In human cleverness (or wisdom), what kinds of things might the natural man think he could do to gain salvation and succeed in life?

   b. What did God do with this kind of wisdom? (v. 20) How? (v. 21)

2. What do verses 18 and 24 say the message (or word) of the cross is to those who are saved? Explain this.

3. What kind of wisdom were the Corinthians obviously following: the wisdom of the world or the wisdom of God (the word of the cross)? How do you know this?

    a. How does James 3:13-16 confirm this?

    b. What do you think Paul was trying to communicate to his friends in this passage so far (vv. 18-25)?

4. God not only chose to use a *method* to save man that would baffle him, but He even chose and called *things* (people) that would be despised to the natural man. List the things God has and has not chosen.

   He has not chosen (v. 26)

   He has chosen (v. 27-28)

    a. Why did God do this?

Making It Personal
The Corinthians had a superiority complex. They thought it was all about them! But Paul reminded them of the real truth of the matter—that by and large they were nothing when they were called into the kingdom of God. Not many of them were wise—some, but not many. Not many were mighty, not many were noble. We must admit the same was true of us! But Jesus, whose teachings are a paradox to the human mind, gives us the right perspective.

5. Read the amazing words Jesus spoke to His disciples in the Sermon on the Mount in Matthew 5 and fill in the following statements:

*Blessed are*_____

*For*_____. (v. 3)

*Blessed are*_____
*For*_____. (v. 4)

*Blessed are*_____
*For*_____.(v. 5)

*Blessed are*_____
*For*_____. (v. 6)

*Blessed are*_____
*For*_____. (v. 7)

*Blessed are*_____
*For*_____. (v. 8)

*Blessed are*_____
*For*_____. (v. 9)

*Blessed are*_____
*For*_____. (v. 10)

*Blessed are*_____
*For*_____. (v. 11-12)

   a. Is this your normal way of looking at things? What message do these words of Jesus have for you today?

Digging Deeper~
✤ Do your best to summarize today's passage in a couple of sentences.

Day 4
Overview of 1 Corinthians 1
Today we will be looking at the passage we have studied this week as a whole. The goal is to find the main lessons the Lord has for us from this chapter. Don't worry about being clever or profound—just do your best!

Find the Facts …

1. See if you can state the <u>content</u> of this week's passage in a couple of sentences. You can use your daily summary statements to help you come up with one main theme or summary of the chapter. (Who is speaking, what is taking place, what is the main subject?)

Look for the Heart …

2. What do you think is the main <u>lesson</u> of this chapter? (What spiritual truths are taught here? Look for a command, a word of exhortation, a promise, etc.)

Hear Him Speak …

3. Look for a <u>personal application</u> from the content of this chapter. It should come from the lesson you got from the chapter (question 2). How will you apply the lesson to yourself?

4. Was there a particular verse that ministered to you this week? What was it and how did it minister to you?

5. Write out your memory verse *from memory*!

NOTES

FIRST CORINTHIANS: *THE WISDOM OF GOD*
LESSON 2
1 CORINTHIANS 2

Paul begins 1 Corinthians 2 with a continuation of his thought process in 1:18-31, where he contrasts the wisdom of the world with the wisdom of God. According to Paul in God's inspired Word, the wisest man who lives by the wisdom of the world will not find God. It is in the apparent foolishness of the cross that the power of God is revealed and received. Paul begins this chapter by sharing his own personal testimony as to how he approached the Corinthians, leaning not on his intellect and powers of persuasion, but on the power of the Holy Spirit. The theme of the chapter is *reliance on the Spirit*.

Day 1
Read 1 Corinthians 2:1-5

1. When Paul first came to Corinth, fulfilling his commission from God, what methods *might* he have used to convince them of the importance of his message?

    1:17

    2:1

    2:4a

    a. Share what this means in simple terms.

2. What was Paul's message? v. 2

a. Does this mean that Paul shared nothing but this one thought, with no personal thoughts or words of explanation? What does it mean?

3. Of what was Paul's message a demonstration? v. 4

    a. How (explain)?

    b. Why? v. 5

We remember that Paul is writing this because of the "party spirit" in the Corinthian church. From the start, we see that Paul did nothing to add to or create this problem. He did everything to see to it that they placed their faith correctly—not in the cleverness of man but in the power of God, who alone brings salvation.

    c. What can happen when a person places their faith and hope in another person rather than on the unchanging God?

Making It Personal
When Paul preached the gospel, what he was really doing was sharing his testimony. He had been saved from death and hell because of Jesus Christ's death on the cross, and he knew that was the point!

4. When sharing your testimony, do you rely more on your exposition than on the power of God? How can you lean on the Spirit more as you share Christ with others?

    a. Share your testimony here with *Jesus Christ and Him crucified* being the main emphasis.

LESSON 2

Digging Deeper
Paul first came to Corinth on his second missionary journey. After revisiting some areas he had been to on his first journey, the Spirit of the Lord led him to the European Continent for the first time.

✢ Trace Paul's journey to Corinth as he traveled through the following cities. If you are able, you may read all of Acts 16-17 to get the entire picture. Look up the following Scriptures and state in a few words the outcome of each visit:

Philippi—Acts 16:19-24

Thessalonica—Acts 17:5, 8-10

Berea—Acts 17:13-14

Athens—Acts 17:32-34

Upon arriving in Corinth, 1 Corinthians 2:3 tells us that Paul was with them "in weakness and in fear and in much trembling." The above verses may give you some understanding as to why that might have been.

Acts 18:1 says, "After these things he left Athens and went to Corinth." There the word of the Lord came, "Do not be afraid, but speak ..." (Acts 18:9 NKJV).

✢ Do your best to summarize today's passage in a couple of sentences.

Memory Verse
"But may it never be that I should boast, except in the cross of our Lord Jesus Christ ..." Galatians 6:14a.

Day 2
Read 1 Corinthians 2:6-10

Paul's thoughts so far almost seem to indicate that he would use *no* wisdom among the Corinthians and that the message of Christ and Him crucified was literally a "foolish" message (rather than a profound and divine message which only *seemed* foolish to the perishing). Of course that was not true. The contrast he makes continues to be between the wisdom of the world and the wisdom of God.

Although Paul was careful to use plain words to preach the message of the cross, so that his audience would not be tempted to rely on the wisdom of man, he does speak words of wisdom to those who are mature.

1. What kind of a person is Paul referring to when he uses the word *mature*? (Does it have anything to do with age or education?) You may use v. 10 to help you with your answer.

    a. Use the following verses to define the wisdom Paul speaks to the mature:

        v. 6 (*negative perspective*)

        v. 6 (*negative perspective*)

        v. 7 (*positive perspective*)

Paul speaks of this wisdom of God as a *mystery*. The usual meaning of the word mystery implies *knowledge withheld*, in the scriptural sense it is *truth revealed*. The New Living Translation speaks of the *secret wisdom of God* (v. 7), hidden in former times, still hidden to many.

2. In Matthew 11:25, Jesus' words emphasize what Paul has spoken so far to the Corinthians. To whom does Jesus say God's mysteries would be hidden? To whom would they be revealed?

    a. How does Mark 10:14-15 amplify this thought?

    b. Share what you think this means.

3. Who *didn't* understand this mystery? 1 Corinthians 2:8

a. What is our proof of this fact?

b. Who do you think Paul was referring to when he spoke of *the rulers of this age*? (Be specific.)

In this passage, we see the *mature* in contrast to the *rulers of this age, Paul's message of wisdom* in contrast to the *wisdom of the age,* and that those who are *not mature* are *unbelievers,* while the *mature* are *believers.*

4. How is it that the mature (those who are believers) know these things that are hidden to others? v. 10

Making It Personal
5. Consider the words in verse 9 (as quoted from Isaiah 64:4). Let your mind go with this verse for a moment. Meditate on the magnificence of God's plan for **you** by way of the cross of Christ.

a. What is Paul's prayer for **you** in Ephesians 1:18?

b. What does Paul want you to know in Ephesians 1:19?

c. Do you get it? Share your thoughts.

Digging Deeper
✤ Do your best to summarize today's passage in a couple of sentences.

✤ What would you consider as the key verse of this passage? Why?

Day 3
Read 1 Corinthians 2:11-16

In these verses, Paul gives us a picture of two types of people—those with the Holy Spirit and those without the Holy Spirit.

In verse 12, Paul makes the most wonderful pronouncement. He says, "Now we have received … the Spirit who is from God." The New Living Translation puts it this way: "God has actually given us His Spirit."

1. What do the following verses teach you on this note?

    Romans 8:9

    1 Corinthians 6:19

    2 Corinthians 1:21-22

Alan Redpath says, "Every child of God has living within him God the Holy Spirit—not an influence, but the Third Person of the Trinity. Therefore every Christian—no matter how weak and feeble, how poor and helpless, perhaps with a sense of utter inability and frustration—whatever his own personal feeling may be, is indwelt by the Third Person of the Trinity."

  a. Personalize these thoughts—make them your own.

2. What do you have that the non-Christian doesn't have? (See 1 Cor. 2:12.)

  a. What difference does this make? v. 14

  b. Share your personal experience with this truth.

3.	What amazing truth does Paul share in verse 16b?

a.	Share the beautiful way this is presented in John 15:15.

Making It Personal
You may not understand everything there is to know about God and His incredible plan for mankind, but if you are a Christian you have the capacity to understand things that are hidden to non-Christians. Each time you pick up the Word, ask the Holy Spirit to open it up to you and to reveal to you the *deep things of God*. Each day, ask the Holy Spirit to fill you and to lead you into all the truth. Ask the Holy Spirit to use you to speak to others and to open up their minds to things of the Spirit. Remind yourself often that as a Christian, you are a *spiritually alive* person—the Holy Spirit dwells in you and that you have the mind of Christ—God can (and does) speak to and through you!

Digging Deeper
✣ Paul has told us that as believers we have the Spirit of God! In His final words to the disciples before the cross, Jesus spoke of the work of the Holy Spirit. Share from these verses the facts Jesus wants you to know (use the NLT if you have it):

John 14:26

John 16:7-8

John 16:13-15

✣ Do your best to summarize today's passage in a couple of sentences.

Day 4

Overview of 1 Corinthians 2

Today we will be looking at the passage we have studied this week as a whole. The goal is to find the main lessons the Lord has for us from this chapter. Don't worry about being clever or profound—just do your best!

Find the Facts ...

1. See if you can state the <u>content</u> of this week's passage in a couple of sentences. You can use your daily summary statements to help you come up with one main theme or summary of the chapter. (Who is speaking, what is taking place, what is the main subject?)

Look for the Heart ...

2. What do you think is the main <u>lesson</u> of this chapter? (What spiritual truths are taught here? Look for a command, a word of exhortation, a promise, etc.)

Hear Him Speak ...

3. Look for a <u>personal application</u> from the content of this chapter. It should come from the lesson you got from the chapter (question 2). How will you apply the lesson to yourself?

4. Was there a particular verse that ministered to you this week? What was it and how did it minister to you?

5. Write out your memory verse *from memory*!

NOTES

FIRST CORINTHIANS: *THE WISDOM OF GOD*
LESSON 3
1 CORINTHIANS 3
⚜

In chapter 2, Paul spoke of two types of people: those with the Holy Spirit and those without. Those with the Spirit are believers; those without the Spirit are non-believers. In our chapter this week, we again see two types of people, but this time Paul is speaking of two types of *believers*: those who are *controlled* by the Spirit and those who are not. Paul calls the one who is controlled by the Spirit *spiritual* and the one who is not *carnal* or *fleshly*. The Corinthian church, according to Paul, is carnal, controlled by their flesh.

Day 1
Read 1 Corinthians 3:1-9

1. In verses 1-3, through his words to the Corinthian church, Paul gives us a *picture* of the carnal Christian. List the things that describe this type of Christian:

2. What example does Paul again point to as evidence that this church is carnal? v. 4

3. People love to have heroes. We love to make celebrities. But Paul and Apollos weren't celebrities. What word did Paul use to describe his position among the Corinthians? v. 5

4. In Matthew 20:25-28, Jesus gives us the concept of servant-leadership:

    a. What perspective does He give the one who desires to be great?

b. How was Jesus our example in this?

5. Paul and Apollos each had a task in regard to the church at Corinth (1 Cor. 3:6):

a. What was Paul's job? (What does this mean?)

b. What was Apollos' job? (What does this mean?)

c. Who caused the growth in this church? Explain this principle. (You may see John 15:4-5.)

Making It Personal (Answer only one.)
⚜ For the person in leadership: From what you have studied today, how will you look at your position? Are there any changes you need to make in your leadership perspective as a result of today's study?

⚜ For the person who would like to be a leader: What insight has today's lesson given you into what it is to be a leader? Is there anything you can do now to prepare yourself for leadership?

Paul simplifies the concept of leadership. He shows us that leaders are fellow workers in the service of God. God is the one who accomplishes the work. Oswald Chambers gives us a clue as to our part in the process. He says, "Put yourself in the place where God's Almighty power will come through you." That makes it pretty simple!

Digging Deeper
In Romans 7:14-25, Paul, using his previous experience as an example, gives us a picture of the carnal (or fleshly) Christian. Read this passage and answer these questions:

⚜ Describe the struggle.

✣ Have you been there? Are you there now? Look up these verses for the answer to the dilemma:

Romans 7:25a

Romans 8:6

Galatians 5:16

John 15:4-5

✣ Do your best to summarize today's passage in a couple of sentences.

Memory Verse
"But I say, 'Walk by the Spirit, and you will not carry out the desire of the flesh.'" Galatians 5:16.

Day 2
Read 1 Corinthians 3:10-15

In verse 9, Paul ended with the principle that he and Apollos were fellow workers in the service of God. The analogy he was drawing, at that point, was of the Corinthian church being a field (God's field) and of he and Apollos being the farmers in that field. Paul finishes his thoughts in verse 9 by changing metaphors. Now he will look at the church as a building (God's building). Both metaphors point to the fact that the Corinthian church belonged to God and that God was their ultimate leader.

1. In verse 10, Paul calls himself a wise master builder who, by the grace of God, laid a foundation among the Corinthians. What was the foundation he laid? v. 11 (You may also see 1 Corinthians 2:2.)

2. In Matthew 16:16, what was the testimony of Peter concerning Jesus Christ?

   a. From the following verses, what did Jesus say about Peter's words?

Matthew 16:17

Matthew 16:18a

   b. Some have taken this to mean that *Peter* would be the foundation of the church. How does 1 Corinthians 3:11 disprove this theory?

   c. What do you think it was in this Matthew passage (16:15-18) that Jesus was referring to when He said, "Upon this rock I will build My church?"

3. Paul gives a strong warning to the leaders of the Corinthian church and to those in church leadership today. What is his warning? v. 10b

   a. How does verse 12 help you understand the concept of building carefully?

   b. Is verse 12 referring to the quantity of Christian work or the quality? What does this mean to you?

   c. In this chapter, Paul is speaking to carnal Christians, controlled by their flesh versus spiritual Christians, controlled by the Holy Spirit. How does this thought help you to understand the different ways one can approach Christian work?

Making It Personal

4. According to verse 13, every one's work will eventually be tested, revealing its quality. The word for "reveal" speaks of *taking off the cover*. On the Day of Judgment, the cover will be taken off and things will be seen as they really are.

a. In regard to both your Christian service and your walk with the Lord, what are your motives:

⚜ To be seen by others?

⚜ To be pleasing to God?

b. When you consider serving others, where is your heart:

⚜ Love for God and for His body?

⚜ Fear of not doing enough or not being accepted by God?

c. Upon whom are you dependent for your service and for your personal Christian growth:

⚜ Yourself?

⚜ God's Spirit?

d. Are you building predominantly with gold, silver, and precious stones, or wood, hay, and straw? Note any changes you might need to make in your *thinking* in order to have the proper perspective in your Christian life and service.

Digging Deeper

⚜ On that day when our works will be tested by fire, it is probable that most of us will suffer some loss, but we will also be rewarded! Look up the following verses which speak of heavenly reward:

Matthew 16:27

Matthew 25:21, 23

1 Corinthians 4:5b

Colossians 3:23-24

Ephesians 6:8

Hebrews 11:6

✤ Do your best to summarize today's passage in a couple of sentences.

Day 3
Read 1 Corinthians 3:16-23

Later in his letter to the Corinthians, Paul speaks to them of the fact that they are *individually* indwelt by God's Holy Spirit (1 Cor. 6:19). But here in 1 Corinthians 3:16, the word he uses for *you* is plural. Paul is speaking here of the collective church at Corinth. The very nature of the *church* is that it is the dwelling place of God.

One commentator said, "Corinth boasted many pagan temples and shrines, but there was only one temple for God—the Corinthian Christians were it!" (Life Application Bible Commentary)

1. What difference might it have made for this divisive, celebrity-oriented church to realize that, as a body, they were the dwelling place of God?

The Amplified Bible translates 1 Corinthians 3:16 this way: "Do you not discern and understand that you [the whole church at Corinth] are God's temple (His sanctuary), and that God's Spirit has His permanent dwelling in you [to be at home in you, collectively as a church and also individually]?"

2. What will happen to the one who defiles God's temple, the church? v. 17

   a. Why?

In verses 18-20, Paul returns to the theme of *wisdom*, tying his thoughts to that which has gone before. We realize that it was the *worldly wisdom* of this *worldly church* that was in danger of defiling it. Remember again Paul's warning in verse 10, "Be careful how you build." The Corinthians weren't being careful at all. They were trying to build on the foundation of Jesus Christ with worldly methods and worldly wisdom (wood, hay, and straw).

3. What is God's appraisal of worldly wisdom?

    verse 19

    verse 20

4. In verse 21 Paul says, "So then ..." So then *what*?

5. If you, in Christ, are the temple of the Holy Spirit, what does Paul (or Apollos, or Cephas, or anyone else) have that you don't have? Explain.

    a. List the things that Paul says belong to this Corinthian church (and to you as a Christian): v. 22

It's interesting to see things turned around from the way the Corinthians had been looking at them. They didn't belong to the church leaders they were following, those leaders belonged to them! Paul and Apollos were *their* servants, as was every other thing pertaining to life—servants of the Christian.

    b. How does Paul express this same wonderful idea in Romans 8:38-39?

Making It Personal
The Amplified Bible translates 1 Corinthians 3:22-23 this way: "Whether Paul or Apollos or Cephas (Peter), or the universe or life or death, or the immediate and threatening present, or the [subsequent and uncertain] future—all are yours."

6. How do the thoughts of Paul in verses 21-23 and Romans 8:38-39 give you hope and courage as you live in this uncertain world and time?

Digging Deeper

✤ Do your best to summarize today's passage in a couple of sentences.

✤ See if you can summarize the heart of this entire chapter.

Day 4
Overview of 1 Corinthians 3

Today we will be looking at the passage we have studied this week as a whole. The goal is to find the main lessons the Lord has for us from this chapter. Don't worry about being clever or profound—just do your best!

Find the Facts …

1. See if you can state the <u>content</u> of this week's passage in a couple of sentences. You can use your daily summary statements to help you come up with one main theme or summary of the chapter. (Who is speaking, what is taking place, what is the main subject?)

Look for the Heart …

2. What do you think is the main <u>lesson</u> of this chapter? (What spiritual truths are taught here? Look for a command, a word of exhortation, a promise, etc.)

Hear Him Speak ...

3. Look for a <u>personal application</u> from the content of this chapter. It should come from the lesson you got from the chapter (question 2). How will you apply the lesson to yourself?

4. Was there a particular verse that ministered to you this week? What was it and how did it minister to you?

5. Write out your memory verse *from memory*!

NOTES

FIRST CORINTHIANS: *THE WISDOM OF GOD*
LESSON 4
1 CORINTHIANS 4

⚜

Chapter 4 actually finishes up the first section of Paul's letter to the Corinthians, which began in chapter 1 with his appeal for unity. We remember the problem was that the Corinthian church had divided itself into parties, some for Paul, some for Apollos, some for Peter. Those for Paul were, in essence, looking down on those for Apollos. Those for Apollos and Peter would have been looking down on those for Paul. All in all, it was wrong—whether they thought Paul was the best or the worst! In chapter 4, he reminds them again of who he is—on the one hand, simply a servant of Christ, on the other, the very father of their faith.

Day 1
Read 1 Corinthians 4:1-5

1. Paul uses 2 key words to express how he sees his ministry. Consider the meaning of his words and see if you can define what he is communicating about himself. (You may look these words up in a regular dictionary or a Bible dictionary for a clearer meaning.)

✤ Servant(s) of Christ

✤ Steward(s) of the mysteries of God

Even these words give us a sense of the *humility* of the calling. The word *servant* speaks of a subordinate who waits to accomplish the commands of his superior (in this case, Jesus Christ). We also see the *high* calling of his ministry. The word *steward* speaks of a high-ranking servant entrusted with the oversight of a household, managing and distributing the household resources (in this case, the very mysteries of God!).

2. What does Paul say is the particular requirement for his position? v. 2

    a. To whom would the steward be accountable—those to whom he distributed the household goods or to the master of the house?

    b. How did Paul explain his perspective on this in verses 3-4?

    c. Why do you think Paul said this to them?

3. Paul says, "Therefore do not go on passing judgement."

    a. When was "the time" Paul was referring to?

    b. What would the Lord do at that time?

    c. What would be the result?

4. It's interesting that Paul speaks of *each man's praise* coming to him from God. He doesn't say some men's praise but each man's praise. How do Paul's words in Romans 14:4 agree with this thought?

    a. How does this encourage you today?

Making It Personal

We live in a world where, for most of us, it matters very much what other people think. Yet, at the same time, we are very quick to share what we think about others!

5. How has it been a problem for you to be too concerned about human judgments?

    a. Why, again, does Paul not concern himself with the judgments of others?

    b. How might it help you to apply Paul's perspective to your own life?

6. On the other hand, can you completely divorce yourself from the judgments of others? Share your thoughts on how you might maintain a healthy balance.

Digging Deeper

✤ Do your best to summarize today's passage in a couple of sentences.

Memory Verse

"Imitate me, just as I also imitate Christ." 1 Corinthians 11:1 NKJV

Day 2
Read 1 Corinthians 4:6-13

This passage is a difficult one to clearly understand, as Paul uses irony to make his point to the Corinthians. What does stand out in this portion of Scripture is the fact that, although we regard the position of Paul the apostle as of the highest order, in his day it was one of degradation and lowliness. What an amazing thing to realize!

1. Each of the following verses have adjectives describing how the Corinthians seemed to see themselves. See if you can locate these adjectives:

verse 6b

verse 7 (NASB, NLT best)

verse 8

2. Use the adjectives from the following verses to describe Paul and the apostles:

verse 9

verse 10

3. In verse 10, note the contrast Paul sets up between the Corinthians and the apostles, in order to point out the foolishness of the their thinking.

| The Apostles | The Corinthians |

⚜

⚜

⚜

4. From verses 11-12a, describe reality for the apostles.

    a. Are these the conditions you would expect for the apostles—the very ministers of the mysteries of God? Have you seen this to be true of ministers in today's world? Think of any examples you can.

Although Paul used these statements to make a point to the Corinthians of the mistakenness of their boasting, still he presented the truth as it was. And yet, Paul walks in the Spirit not in the flesh ...

5. From verses 12-13:

    ⚜   How did the apostles handle being reviled?

✤ How did they handle persecution?

✤ How did they handle being slandered?

✤ How did Paul describe what they became in order to fulfill their ministry?

Making It Personal

The Corinthians thought too highly of themselves but not according to reality from God's point of view, only according to their own evaluation of things based on the wisdom of the world at that time. How embarrassed they must have been when they read the words Paul wrote.

6. Do you think, in general, Christians today are more like the Corinthians, in all their glory, or like Paul in his degradation?

   a. Have you ever found yourself looking down on someone less fortunate than yourself? How would you feel if you found out that person was sacrificially doing the work of the Lord?

   b. What does the person who is proud in this world fail to realize? (See v. 7)

   c. What do you have that you have not received? If you are going to boast, what does Paul suggest that you boast in? See 1 Corinthians 1:30-31

Digging Deeper

Paul's description of the apostles reminds us of the description of another, namely, Jesus Christ, who said, "The foxes have holes, and the birds of the air have nests, but the Son of Man has nowhere to lay His head" (Luke 9:58). The Bible also speaks of Him as being "despised and forsaken of men, a man of sorrows and acquainted with grief" (Isaiah 53:3a). How quickly we forget our example. How easily we are led to think that our lot should be somehow different and definitely better.

✤ In the following verses, Jesus Himself gives a picture of the one who would follow in His steps:

Matthew 5:3

Matthew 5:4

Matthew 16:24

Matthew 16:25

Matthew 19:21

Paul's thoughts—Philippians 1:29

Peter's thoughts—1 Peter 2:21

The apostles' example—Acts 5:41

Jesus' example—1 Peter 2:23-24

✤ Do your best to summarize today's passage in a couple of sentences.

Day 3
Read 1 Corinthians 4:14-21

1. What gave Paul the right to admonish the Corinthians?

   verse 14

   verse 15 (explain this verse)

2. Because of his position in their lives, how was he able to exhort them? v. 16

a. What further reason did Paul have for being able to exhort them in this manner? 1 Corinthians 11:1

b. If they began to obey this exhortation, how would their behavior be changed? (Remember what we studied yesterday.) What a great perspective this was for them!

3. What provision was Paul making that would help the Corinthians in their effort to *imitate* him and why would this make a difference? v. 17

4. In what way were some of the Corinthians being arrogant about Paul? v. 18 What kinds of things might they have been saying?

a. What was it Paul's plan to do? What would he then learn?

b. How did Paul want to come to them? (Remember verse 14.)

Making It Personal

Paul was able to say to the Corinthians, "Imitate me, just as I also imitate Christ." Paul not only shared the truth with his words, but he also lived it with his life.

5. Would you be able to tell another person that they should imitate you? Consider an area you would need to change in order to be able to exhort another person in this manner.

Digging Deeper

✤ Find out who Timothy was by looking at the following verses, making note of anything that stands out to you along the way:

Timothy the young man: Acts 16:1-2; 2 Timothy 1:5

In ministry with Paul: Acts 16:3a

To Philippi: (they) Acts 16:6-12

To Thessalonica: (they) Acts 17:1

To Berea: (with Paul and Silas) Acts 17:10; 13-15;

At Corinth: (with Paul) Acts 18:4-5

To Ephesus: Acts 18:18-19

At Ephesus: 1 Timothy 1:3

In Paul's heart: Romans 16:21; 1 Cor.4:17; 16:10-11; 1 Tim. 1:1-2 and 2 Tim. 1:1-2

Last personal written words of Paul (to Timothy): 2 Tim. 4:9; 13; 21

✣ Do your best to summarize today's passage in a couple of sentences.

Day 4
Overview of 1 Corinthians 4

Today we will be looking at the passage we have studied this week as a whole. The goal is to find the main lessons the Lord has for us from this chapter. Don't worry about being clever or profound—just do your best!

Find the Facts ...

1. See if you can state the <u>content</u> of this week's passage in a couple of sentences. You can use your daily summary statements to help you come up with one main theme or summary of the chapter. (Who is speaking, what is taking place, what is the main subject?)

Look for the Heart ...

2. What do you think is the main <u>lesson</u> of this chapter? (What spiritual truths are taught here? Look for a command, a word of exhortation, a promise, etc.)

Hear Him Speak ...

3. Look for a <u>personal application</u> from the content of this chapter. It should come from the lesson you got from the chapter (question 2). How will you apply the lesson to yourself?

4. Was there a particular verse that ministered to you this week? What was it and how did it minister to you?

5. Write out your memory verse *from memory*!

NOTES

FIRST CORINTHIANS: *THE WISDOM OF GOD*
LESSON 5
1 CORINTHIANS 5

⚜

Paul now shifts gears in his letter to the Corinthians to speak to them on some very specific topics. Keep in mind that Paul writes this letter in general to correct and redirect their thinking, particularly and most importantly directing them to keep their focus on Christ. In the next few chapters, we'll see him speak directly on the subject of immorality, beginning with the subject of sexual sin.

Day 1
Read 1 Corinthians 5:1-5

The very words Paul begins with give us a sense of his amazement at what is being allowed to go on. He says, "It is actually reported," in other words, commonly reported, or commonly known. Paul had heard about it—it was common knowledge.

1. As a review, begin by reading 1 Corinthians 4:18-21, connecting Paul's thoughts there with the beginning words of chapter 5.

    ✣ How do you think Paul wanted to come to them?

    ✣ How does it seem he needed to come to them?

    ✣ What gave Paul the authority to come to them with "a rod"?

2. What was the "common" report?

a. Was this a "common" problem?

b. The Jews had very strict laws for this kind of immorality. Look at the following verses for the O.T. law:

Leviticus 18:8

Deuteronomy 22:30

Deuteronomy 27:20

c. What was the bottom line in the law for this kind of sin? Leviticus 20:11

3. What seemed to be the reaction of the Corinthian church to this sin going on in their midst?

4. Although Paul wasn't there with them, what does verse 3 tell us he had already done?

a. What were they to do? vv. 4-5

b. See if you can explain Paul's intention for the one in sin. What do you think it means to:

✤ Deliver him to Satan?

✤ For the destruction of his flesh?

✤ That his spirit would be saved in the day of the Lord Jesus?

Making It Personal

5. Paul says, "You have become arrogant and have not mourned instead ..." James 4:7-10 gives us the ingredients for humility—both in church over sin in the body and for you individually when you realize you have allowed sin in your life:

    Submit _____

    Resist _____

    Draw near _____

    Cleanse _____

    Purify _____

    Be miserable _____

    Let your _____

    Humble _____

    a. Draw a simple conclusion for repentant behavior from these verses.

Digging Deeper

✠ Matthew 18 gives us the blueprint for church discipline. From these verses, share the 3 point plan of confronting sin in the body:

verse 15

verse 16

verse 17

✠ Do your best to summarize today's passage in a couple of sentences.

Memory Verse

"Be miserable and mourn and weep; let your laughter be turned into mourning, and your joy to gloom."
James 4:9

Day 2
Read 1 Corinthians 5:6-8

Alan Redpath says, "We come to grips now with the root of the trouble in the church at Corinth, the sin that ruined its testimony and made their pride in worldly wisdom and human philosophy so blatantly out of place."

Paul says, "Your boasting is not good."

1. Explain how Paul's "little leaven" illustrates the potential of harm to this church because of the sin of this man.

2. How would removing this man from church fellowship have the same effect as *purging out the old leaven*?

3. Paul speaks of them as being in truth *"unleavened"* (verse 7).

   a. Why were they unleavened according to this verse?

   b, What do you think this means?

   c. What is the significance of Christ's death in relationship to their state of being unleavened? See 2 Corinthians 5:17

4. Although most believers don't celebrate the Feast of Unleavened Bread, we do celebrate our "unleavened" state as Christians. How does Paul say we should celebrate our feast? v. 8

   Not with

   Nor with

   But with

a. Explain how the leaven of sincerity and truth would have the same effect as the old leaven, but with a positive result.

Making It Personal

5. How "little" of a sin do you think might be considered a "little leaven"?

Exodus 13:7 says, "And nothing leavened shall be seen among you." In other words, every bit was to be thrown out.

a. Can you afford to leave a "little leaven" in your life? Share.

b. Have you ever really considered the effect your sin has on the rest of the body of Christ? Share your thoughts.

Digging Deeper

Paul speaks in verse 7 of "Christ our Passover." Exodus 12 tells the story of the original Passover as actually experienced by the Jews, which pointed toward the sacrifice of Jesus for our sins.

✤ Read Exodus 12:1-36 and make note of the important elements of the original Passover instructions and procedures.

✤ Where do you see Christ in this story?

✤ Where do you see yourself in this story?

✣ There is a saying, "you should be what you are." What are *you* now that "Christ our Passover has been sacrificed"?

✣ Do your best to summarize today's passage in a couple of sentences.

Day 3
Read 1 Corinthians 5:9-13

Paul speaks of a letter written before—the letter he refers to is the *real* 1 Corinthians, the letter *we* call 1 Corinthians is actually the second letter Paul wrote to the Corinthians! The letter Paul refers to here is often called the "lost letter" because it wasn't preserved.

1. How did Paul differentiate between those the church *were* to judge and those they *were not* to judge?

    a. Whose job is it to judge non-believers?

    b. Whose job is it to judge those inside the church?

    c. See if you can explain this concept.

2. In chapter 4, Paul spoke of *not passing judgment before the time*, saying that *the Lord* would disclose the motives of men's hearts.

✣ What kind of judgment is Paul talking about in chapter 4?

✤ What kind of judgment is he talking about in chapter 5?

✤ What is the difference?

3. Paul not only speaks of sexual immorality here, but in verse 11 he gives a list of other sins. See if you can define the other sins mentioned by Paul:

covetousness—

idolatry—

revelry—

drunkenness—

extortion—

   a. How complete is the separation to be from the one who continues in unrepentant sin? v. 11b

Making It Personal

4. As Christians, are we to be detectives, or in other words sin-sniffers? Share your thoughts.

   a. Taking in all you have read so far this week, see if you can share from a personal place how you will respond if it comes to you that a brother or sister is in sin? Ephesians 4:32a

Note: There isn't a perfect or exactly "right" way to handle these things. Bathed in prayer and led by the Spirit, we take the teaching of the word and speak the truth in love (Ephesians 4:15 with Ephesians 4:32 in mind.

Digging Deeper

✤ Do your best to summarize today's passage in a couple of sentences.

LESSON 5

Day 4
Overview of 1 Corinthians 5

Today we will be looking at the passage we have studied this week as a whole. The goal is to find the main lessons the Lord has for us from this chapter. Don't worry about being clever or profound—just do your best!

Find the Facts ...

1. See if you can state the content of this week's passage in a couple of sentences. You can use your daily summary statements to help you come up with one main theme or summary of the chapter. (Who is speaking, what is taking place, what is the main subject?)

Look for the Heart ...

2. What do you think is the main lesson of this chapter? (What spiritual truths are taught here? Look for a command, a word of exhortation, a promise, etc.)

Hear Him Speak ...

3. Look for a personal application from the content of this chapter. It should come from the lesson you got from the chapter (question 2). How will you apply the lesson to yourself?

4. Was there a particular verse that ministered to you this week? What was it and how did it minister to you?

5. Write out your memory verse *from memory*!

NOTES

FIRST CORINTHIANS: *THE WISDOM OF GOD*
LESSON 6
1 CORINTHIANS 6
⚜

In chapter 5, it was "reported" that there was sexual immorality going on, and so, in chapter 6, we must assume it was also "reported" that the Corinthian Christians were suing each other in public courts of law. Paul is amazed, as we can see in verse 1. This chapter is actually a continuation of the thoughts begun in chapter 5, discussing the general moral laxity of the Christians in Corinth—those that God had redeemed by the very blood of His own dear Son, the "called out ones," who were living as if they had not been called out but were part of the pagan culture in which they lived.

Day 1
Read 1 Corinthians 6:1-8

Verse 1 begins with the words, "*Does* any of you ... dare ...?" We can almost hear Paul saying, "*How* dare you!"

1. What were these Corinthian Christians *daring* to do? Explain what they were doing in everyday terms.

2. According to verse 1, as a Christian, to whom should you take your disputes?

    a. If you were in such a situation today, how would you do this?

3. Why should the saints be qualified to judge temporal (trivial) matters?

    verse 2a

verse 3a

Paul speaks of the Corinthians appointing those "of no account in the church" to judge (verse 4). The NKVJ calls them the "least esteemed." This has been understood to mean either men of little account in the church (in other words, believers who were not thought highly of), or it may have meant non-believers.

4.   Who would you think of as being more qualified to judge your Christian dispute: the least esteemed Christian in your church or a wise and learned non-believer? Explain why.

   a.   What would you think if you took your dispute to the church and they judged wrongly?

   b.   What does verse 7 say about this?

   c.   Consider why it was a shame (v. 5) for them to behave this way—why it would be better to be wronged.

Making It Personal

A man named Herman Ridderbos has said, "For the sake of the kingdom, Jesus wants His disciples to give up their rights, interests, benefits and safeguards ..." (Holman New Testament Commentary, I & II Corinthians.)

5.   How does the cross of Christ apply to the passage we have studied today?

   a.   Are you more careful about your personal rights or about the kingdom of God? Share your thoughts.

   b.   Is there something you have been fighting for that you should lay down today for the kingdom of God, rather than insisting upon your own rights?

Digging Deeper

✤ Paul speaks in this passage of believers judging the world and judging angels. The following verses give us the background for his statements.

Judging the world: Matthew 19:28; 2 Timothy 2:12a; Jude 14-15; Revelation 3:21; 20:4a

Judging angels: 2 Peter 2:4; Jude 6, Revelation 19:19-20; 20:10

✤ Do your best to summarize today's passage in a couple of sentences.

Memory Verse

"I have been crucified with Christ; and it is no longer I who live, but Christ lives in me; and the life which I now live in the flesh I live by faith in the Son of God, who loved me and delivered Himself up for me." Galatians 2:20

Day 2
Read 1 Corinthians 6:9-11

1. What were some of the Corinthians before Christ? vv. 9-11a

The list Paul gives of sins in this chapter is most likely correspondent to the problems in the Corinthian church. Sexual immorality was rampant in Corinth. Homosexuality and male prostitution were especially characteristic of the Greco-Roman society. Temple prostitution was the norm and was linked in their culture with worship.

2. What had been done for them "in Christ"? v. 11

3. What do the following verses say about these elements of our salvation?

Washed—John 15:3; Titus 3:5; Hebrews 10:22; Revelation 7:14

Sanctified—John 17:17; 1 Corinthians 1:2; 1 Thessalonians 4:3; 5:23; 1 Peter 1:2

Justified—Romans 3:24; 5:1; 8:1(implied)

Making It Personal

4. What were *you* before Christ washed, sanctified, and justified you?

    a. Which aspect of your salvation found in verse 11 is dearest to your heart and why?

Digging Deeper

✤ With verse 7 ("Why do you not rather accept wrong?") and 11 ("And such were some of you.") in mind, consider Jesus' parable of the Unmerciful Servant in Matthew 18:21-35. Share your thoughts.

✤ Do your best to summarize today's passage in a couple of sentences.

Day 3
Read 1 Corinthians 6:12-20

Verse 12 connects the thoughts that have gone before with the rest of the chapter. All things are lawful, Paul says: you *can* take your Christian brother to the courts of the non-believers—but is it *helpful* (NKJV) or *profitable* (NASB)? No! We have been cleansed, we have been sanctified, we have been justified, we have been redeemed by the precious blood of the Lamb; are we to continue living to please ourselves?

1. What do you think Paul meant when he said that as a Christian all things are lawful to him?

a. Although all things are lawful to the believer Paul, his greater concern is what is profitable. What exactly does he mean?

b. What do you think Paul meant when he said that although all things were lawful to him, he would not be *mastered* (NASB) by anything?

2. Throughout verses 13-19, Paul emphasizes who we belong to, as Christians. How does he say this in these verses? (Personalize it with, *My or I...*)

verse 13

verse 15

verse 17

verse 19

3. In Corinth, at the time Paul wrote this, temple prostitution was a part of the worship ritual. How do these verses make it clear that, as a Christian, sexual immorality is strictly banned?

verse 13

verse 15-16

verse 18

4. How does Paul conclude his thoughts on all immorality as addressed in chapter 6? v. 20

Making It Personal
5. Is there anything in your life of which it might be said that you are not glorifying God? Think this over carefully. (Although all things are lawful—those things that are not strictly forbidden in Scripture—all things are not profitable, nor are all things glorifying to God.) Name anything the Holy Spirit identifies to you here.

a. What should you do? See Paul's words in 1 Corinthians 9:24-27.

Digging Deeper
✣ Tie this week's memory verse (Galatians 2:20) with the heart of what Paul is saying in this chapter.

Day 4
Overview of 1 Corinthians 6
Today we will be looking at the passage we have studied this week as a whole. The goal is to find the main lessons the Lord has for us from this chapter. Don't worry about being clever or profound—just do your best!

Find the Facts ...
1. See if you can state the <u>content</u> of this week's passage in a couple of sentences. You can use your daily summary statements to help you come up with one main theme or summary of the chapter. (Who is speaking, what is taking place, what is the main subject?)

Look for the Heart ...
2. What do you think is the main <u>lesson</u> of this chapter? (What spiritual truths are taught here? Look for a command, a word of exhortation, a promise, etc.)

Hear Him Speak ...
3. Look for a <u>personal application</u> from the content of this chapter. It should come from the lesson you got from the chapter (question 2). How will you apply the lesson to yourself?

4. Was there a particular verse that ministered to you this week? What was it and how did it minister to you?

5. Write out your memory verse *from memory*!

NOTES

FIRST CORINTHIANS: *THE WISDOM OF GOD*
LESSON 7
1 CORINTHIANS 7:1-24
❧

Chapter 7 begins the section of this letter in which Paul answers specific questions asked by the Corinthian believers. The first question appears to have been about marriage. This is one of those difficult chapters that we often want to circumvent, but we are going to go right through it this week, with the determination to know what *God* says about marriage and remarriage.

One thing to remember as we proceed is that *you are where you are today*. I always remember the wise words of my Bible Study Fellowship teacher when teaching a passage on divorce. She said, "You can't unscramble eggs." I've always remembered that. As we move through this difficult study, accept God's words as truth, but also accept the fact that we are weak creatures. That's why we need a Savior! And remember the comforting words of Paul: "Therefore there is now no condemnation for those who are in Christ Jesus." Romans 8:1

Day 1
Read 1 Corinthians 7:1-7

1. What was Paul's stand on celibacy (the state of not being married; abstention from sexual intercourse)? v. 1

   a. How did Paul see celibacy as it applied to him and others like him? v. 7

   b. Why do you think Paul regarded celibacy in this way? See 1 Cor. 7:32-34a

   c. How did Jesus say this? Matthew 19:10-12

Although Paul begins with a word on celibacy (probably in answer to a specific question), his emphasis in this section is not on celibacy but on marriage.

2. What is one reason that it is better for men and women to marry. v. 2

    a. What is God's viewpoint on marriage? Genesis 2:18

We learned in the last two chapters (5 and 6) that immorality was a big problem in Corinth. It seems there were those who took things to the opposite extreme saying that *all* sexual relations were bad and that abstinence should be practiced even in marriage.

3. What is Paul's response to this viewpoint?

   verse 3

   verse 4

   verse 5a

4. What is the only exception Paul gives for abstaining from sex in the marriage relationship? v. 5

    a. What warning does Paul give in the case of this exception? v. 5b

    b. In your own words, what is Paul's fear for the married couple that does not continue fulfilling each other's physical needs?

Making It Personal

In the early days of marriage, a couple is very aware of the needs of their spouse. But when the years go by and the difficulties of life press in, recognizing and caring for the needs of the other may go by the wayside. Rather than thinking from the negative perspective of fulfilling a *duty*, it might help to get the positive perspective of *caring*, realizing that what 1 Corinthians 7:3-5 teaches is that married couples have a responsibility to *care* for each other.

5. *Whether you are married or single*: How has the Lord spoken to you in today's portion of Scripture?

Digging Deeper
✤ Look at the following verses that tell us what the Bible—therefore God Himself—says about marriage:

Genesis 2:18 and 24

Matthew 19:6

Romans 7:2-3

1 Corinthians 7:4

Ephesians 5:21-25

Ephesians 5:33

Hebrews 13:4

✤ Do your best to summarize today's passage in a couple of sentences.

Memory Verse
"So take heed to your spirit, that you do not deal treacherously." Malachi 2:16b

Day 2
Read 1 Corinthians 7:8-16

Paul gives instructions in this section for three possible situations: 1) people who are unmarried; 2) Christians married to Christians; 3) Christians married to unbelievers.

1. What does Paul say to the unmarried and widows? v. 8

    a. What does he mean, exactly?

    b. What exception does he give? v. 9

2. What instruction is given to those in marriages where both parties are Christians? v. 10

    a. Whose instruction is this, according to this verse?

    b. If a woman decides to leave her Christian husband, what is her recourse? v. 11

    c. What was Jesus' word on this? Matthew 5:32

3. What instruction is given to Christians married to non-believers? vv. 12-13

It's possible that there were some Christians in Corinth who thought it would be advantageous to leave their pagan spouse and marry a Christian. Paul says, "No!"

    a. In verse 14, Paul gives the reason for the Christian to remain with the unbelieving spouse, if that spouse consents—what does he say?

We know that Paul doesn't mean here that the husband or the children will be *saved* by their relationship to the believer. Each person must individually come to Christ and be born again by the Spirit of the Lord.

    b. Share your thoughts on what Paul might mean when he says the unbelieving husband is sanctified and the children made holy.

4. What exception does he give to the believer married to a non-believer? v. 15 Why? v. 15b

Making It Personal

1 Peter 3:1-4 is written particularly for a woman married to an non-believing husband, but it is a beneficial word to every married woman and even to the single woman who one day hopes to be married. Read these verses (the Amplified Bible is best!) and apply them, where you can, to your particular situation.

Digging Deeper

✤ As you read the passage today—God's word on divorce and remarriage—it is obvious that the allowance for room is narrow in either case. What does Malachi 2:16 say is *God's* perspective on divorce.

✤ Share either from a personal experience or your best understanding of why God would say that He hates divorce.

Note: There are exceptions given in the Bible in which case separation and/or divorce are allowed: adultery and abandonment (See Matthew 19:9 and 1 Corinthians 7:15). Also be aware that physical abuse is never condoned. If you are in a situation in which there is abuse, leave the situation and get godly counsel.

✤ Do your best to summarize today's passage in a couple of sentences.

Day 3
Read 1 Corinthians 7:17-24

What we have studied so far has to do with celibacy, marriage, divorce, and remarriage. As a title to the whole chapter, we could take the final verses and summarize with the words, "*Stay Where You Are.*"

1. How does Paul say this in:

    verse 17

    verse 20

    verse 24

2. What examples does Paul give of this principle being true?

    ✤ Example—verse 18

    Why? verse 19

    ✤ Example—verse 21

    Why? v. 22

    a. How does Paul's principle of *staying where you are* apply to:

        ✤ the unmarried—v. 8

        ✤ married Christians—v. 10

        ✤ Christians married to non-believers—v. 13

3. What would be the only exception to the principle of *staying where you are* when you come to the Lord?

Making It Personal

In *marriage* there is no question (except in the very specific cases already mentioned)—God says stay put! But there *are* areas in life in which you may have a choice to move or to stay.

4. Is there a situation in your life that you've been trying to find a way out of, but to no avail? Could it be that God is asking you to *stay where you are*?

    a.   There is a saying, *"Bloom where you're planted."* What does this mean to you in your life today?

Digging Deeper

✣ Do your best to summarize today's passage in a couple of sentences.

Day 4

Overview of 1 Corinthians 7:1-24

Today we will be looking at the passage we have studied this week as a whole. The goal is to find the main lessons the Lord has for us from this chapter. Don't worry about being clever or profound—just do your best!

Find the Facts …

1.   See if you can state the <u>content</u> of this week's passage in a couple of sentences. You can use your daily summary statements to help you come up with one main theme or summary of the chapter. (Who is speaking, what is taking place, what is the main subject?)

Look for the Heart …

2.   What do you think is the main <u>lesson</u> of this chapter? (What spiritual truths are taught here? Look for a command, a word of exhortation, a promise, etc.)

Hear Him Speak …

3. Look for a <u>personal application</u> from the content of this chapter. It should come from the lesson you got from the chapter (question 2). How will you apply the lesson to yourself?

4. Was there a particular verse that ministered to you this week? What was it and how did it minister to you?

5. Write out your memory verse *from memory*!

NOTES

FIRST CORINTHIANS: *THE WISDOM OF GOD*
LESSON 8
1 CORINTHIANS 7:25-40
❧

In the second half of chapter 7, Paul continues his theme of *staying where you are*. At this point, though, it seems that he is not speaking from the perspective of fulfilling your duty or vows but of serving the kingdom of God—giving the Corinthians an *eternal perspective*.

Parts of this passage need to be seen in the light of the times. 1 Corinthians has been called an "occasional" document, because it is specifically tied to the immediate circumstances of the church addressed. It has also been said that, in some cases, answers to questions were "occasional" answers or "occasional" advice, tailored to the Corinthian's particular situation. So, we must take that into consideration as we study this portion of Scripture.

The true heart of this passage has to do with the expedience of serving the kingdom of God while there is time!

Day 1
Read 1 Corinthians 7:25-28

The NLT translates the first part of verse 25, "Now about the young women who are not yet married." The Greek word for *virgin* in this verse is *parthenos* and means a maiden, by implication an unmarried daughter, a virgin. When Paul speaks of a virgin in this passage, he is speaking of an unmarried daughter or, in other words, a young girl who has never been married. When he speaks of an unmarried woman, he is speaking of a woman who has previously been married.

1. What is Paul's word to *marriageable maidens* (Amplified)? vv. 25-26

    a. Is this a command from the Lord? What is it? What *reason* does Paul give for giving such advice? v. 26

b.   Why does Paul feel he is in a position to give such advice?

It is not completely clear what the impending or present distress was in verse 26. It is thought that these words may refer to the soon second coming of Christ, or to the persecution of the church that was imminent, or to a possible famine in the area at that time.

2.   Here again, we have Paul's overall thought in chapter 7, "it is good for a man to remain as he is."

✤ What is Paul's advice to the married? v. 27

✤ What is Paul's advice the unmarried? v.27

In each case, Paul uses three specific words: "Do not seek …"

✤ With Matthew 6:33 in mind, apply these three words to your marital state today.

Paul is already attempting to give perspective with these words. He is pulling their eyes off of their present situation and their attempts to fulfill their own personal desires (whether that is seeking to be married or to find a way out of marriage), and onto what really matters.

3.   Does Paul think it is a sin to marry? What is his purpose in writing these things to the Corinthians at this time? v. 28

The Greek word for trouble is *thlipsis* and means pressure, affliction, anguish, burden, persecution, tribulation, and trouble.

a.   If you are married or have been married, you know Paul's words in verse 28 are a fact. There is *trouble* that comes with marriage. Without looking at marriage from a negative perspective, simply from a realistic one, share some of the *troubles* that accompany marriage.

Making It Personal
Most people at some point in their lives think that marriage will solve their problems and bring them continual happiness. Of course, this is not true! Married people still have periods of unhappiness, temptation to sin, personal need, life difficulty, and even loneliness. The answer to the married and the single alike is *contentment* with your life, as it is, and *focusing on Jesus*.

4. Consider those two points and share whether you are:

Content with your life—*see Philippians 4:11-13*

Focusing on Christ—*see Hebrews 12:1-2a*

Digging Deeper

✤ Consider Matthew 6:33 and Colossians 3:1-2 and share your thoughts on having an eternal perspective rather than an earthly one.

✤ Do your best to summarize today's passage in a couple of sentences.

Memory Verse

"Set your mind on the things above, not on the things that are on earth." Colossians 3:2

Day 2
Read 1 Corinthians 7:29-35

As we read today's verses, we must try to gain Paul's perspective. He is answering a specific question: possibly whether or not Christian parents should give their daughters in marriage. Again, we realize Paul has an eternal perspective in mind, which seems to be that marriage (for the single believer) is not to be the priority—being free to serve God is.

1. John MacArthur, speaking of those believers who are married, says, "There must be a scriptural balance, between fulfilling marriage needs and serving the Lord." Paul begins by making a list of several conditions of life that must not keep us from serving the kingdom of God (vv. 29-31):

✤ What is the priority for those who have wives?

✤ What is the priority for the afflicted?

✣ What is the priority for the blessed?

✣ What is the priority for those with possessions?

✣ What is the priority for those who enjoy the world?

2. What is Paul's reason for having this priority?

verse 29a

verse 31b

   a. What do you think he is referring to here?

3. From verses 32-34:

   a. What is the concern of those who are married?

   b. What is the concern of those who are single?

Making It Personal

4. If you are married, can you say that your concern is *how to please your husband*? How might it make a difference in your marriage if this were so?

   a. If you are single, can you say that your concern is *how you may please the Lord*? How might it make a difference in your life if this were so?

Digging Deeper

✤ Are you married today? Are you sad? Are you happy? Are you enjoying life? Are any of these things (yes—even sadness) keeping you from using every opportunity to serve Christ? How should you be looking at the "conditions of life" in the light of eternity? See Ephesians 5:15-17

✤ Do your best to summarize today's passage in a couple of sentences.

Day 3
Read 1 Corinthians 7:36-40

The section we will consider today is addressed to fathers of unmarried daughters or possibly to fiancés (those engaged to be married).

It seems in verse 36, after considering why it was best for the unmarried to *stay where they are*, Paul comes full circle and reiterates his point, while giving allowance to the Christian parent who is considering the marriage of his daughter.

1. What consideration is given in verse 36?

NKJV speaks of this virgin as being *past the flower of youth*. NIV speaks of her as *getting along in years*. Paul is speaking here to the parent whose daughter is getting older (or the fiancé of a woman who is getting older) who feels marriage is the right thing for the situation. Paul says that it's ok to marry!

a. Although Paul concedes that this father who desires his daughter to marry does not sin—still, what is Paul's opinion?

verse 37

verse 38

2. One last word on marriage is given in verse 39 to widows. What freedom does Paul give to the one whose husband has died?

   a. What is the one "rule" for this marriageable widow?

   b. Considering what Paul has had to say so far in this chapter, what do you think he means by *only in the Lord*?

   c. What, again, is his opinion about the widow remarrying?

      verse 8

      verse 40

3. From the opening thoughts of this lesson:

   ✣ What kind of a letter was this (and what does that mean)?

   ✣ How does this make a difference to how you apply it to your life?

   ✣ What is the general point of Paul here (Paul's heart)?

Making It Personal

4. How has this second half of chapter 7:

   ✣ Helped to give you perspective about your marriage?

   ✣ Helped to give you perspective about your singleness?

✤ Helped to give you an eternal perspective?

Digging Deeper

✤ Do your best to summarize the whole teaching of chapter 7.

Day 4

Overview of 1 Corinthians 7:25-40

Today we will be looking at the passage we have studied this week as a whole. The goal is to find the main lessons the Lord has for us from this chapter. Don't worry about being clever or profound—just do your best!

Find the Facts …

1. See if you can state the <u>content</u> of this week's passage in a couple of sentences. You can use your daily summary statements to help you come up with one main theme or summary of the chapter. (Who is speaking, what is taking place, what is the main subject?)

Look for the Heart …

2. What do you think is the main <u>lesson</u> of this chapter? (What spiritual truths are taught here? Look for a command, a word of exhortation, a promise, etc.)

Hear Him Speak …

3. Look for a <u>personal application</u> from the content of this chapter. It should come from the lesson you got from the chapter (question 2). How will you apply the lesson to yourself?

4. Was there a particular verse that ministered to you this week? What was it and how did it minister to you?

5. Write out your memory verse *from memory*!

NOTES

FIRST CORINTHIANS: *THE WISDOM OF GOD*
LESSON 9
1 CORINTHIANS 8

When you read this chapter you will think it is about meat offered to idols—which it is, but it is also about Christian liberty. In fact, the subject of liberty will continue through chapter 10. However, there is an even more important theme that runs through this chapter, and that is the theme of love. We might entitle this chapter, *Liberty Sifted through Love.*

Day 1
Read 1 Corinthians 8:1-13

We don't know the exact question Paul was asked, but it seems obvious that they wanted an absolute word on the issue of eating meat that had been sacrificed to idols. We can tell from Paul's response that the *strong* Corinthian Christians assumed that their knowledge of God and their understanding of the fact that idols were really nothing gave them the freedom to eat this meat, whether sold at the marketplace or in the actual temple. Paul deals first with the question of their *knowledge*, laying the foundation for his answer to their actual question. It is possible that Paul repeats their own words, as they were written to him, when he says, "we know that we all have knowledge."

1. Even though they "all have knowledge," what, in one word, does Paul see as the priority? v. 1

   a. According to Paul, what does *knowledge* do?

   b. What do you think this means?

2. According to Paul, what does *love* do?

a. Using your dictionary, define the word *edify*.

In the Greek, the word for love is *oikodomeo* and means to be a house-builder, construct, confirm, build, edify, embolden.

b. With these definitions in mind, can you say that you are *loving* anyone in the way Paul speaks of here in chapter 8? Who would you like to begin loving in this way? How can you begin to apply this idea of love *edifying* this very week in your own home? Remember, love is a *house-builder*!

3. That Paul begins with this statement (verse 1) tells us something about these *strong* Corinthian Christians. What does it tell us?

a. To succinctly state what Paul is communicating to them in verse 1 about *knowledge* and *love*, fill in the following statement: To _____ is better than to _____.

Although Paul will soon give them his thoughts on whether or not it is proper for Christians to eat meat sacrificed to idols, first he wants them to understand that *love* rules. They may *know* that idols are nothing (verse 4), but love for others overrules what knowledge may permit: love does not serve knowledge, knowledge serves love.

Because we see in verse 1 that Paul makes a contrast between knowledge and love, with love coming in as superior, we must look at verse 2 in that same light. The Amplified Bible translates it this way: "If anyone imagines that he has come to know and understand much [of divine things, without love], he does not yet perceive and recognize and understand as strongly and clearly, nor has he become as intimately acquainted with anything as he ought or as is necessary."

b. What is Paul trying to say in this verse?

Making It Personal
4. In verse 3, Paul makes the statement that the one who loves God is known by Him. Consider which is more significant, that you know God, or that He knows you.

a. Look at what the Apostle John calls himself in John 13:23. Have you ever thought of yourself in those terms—as the disciple whom Jesus loves? What difference might it make in your relationship to Jesus if you saw yourself from that point of view?

Listen to what J.I. Packer says on this subject: "What matters supremely, therefore, is not, in the last analysis, the fact that I know God, but the larger fact which underlies it—the fact that *He knows me.* I am graven on the palms of His hands; I am never out of His mind. All my knowledge of Him depends on His sustained initiative in knowing me. I know Him because He first knew me and continues to know me. He knows me as a friend ..." Selah!!!

Digging Deeper
✤ Do your best to summarize today's passage in a couple of sentences.

Memory Verse
"Do not use liberty as an opportunity for the flesh, but through love serve one another." Galatians 5:13 NKJV

Day 2
Read 1 Corinthians 8:4-6

1. What stand did the Jerusalem Council take on meat sacrificed to idols? Acts 15:28-29

a. What was Paul's previous word to the Corinthians concerning associating with idolaters? 1 Corinthians 5:9-11

It would seem from these verses that the answer to the question, *"Can a Christian eat meat sacrificed to idols?"* was *"No!"* But we remember again that this was an occasional letter, written to this specific church in this specific Greek area and culture. Paul would stand behind the decision of the Jerusalem Council in general. Obviously, they were not to associate with Christians who actually worshipped idols, but the culture of these Corinthians made it nearly impossible not to come into contact with idolatry, both at the temple, which was the common dining hall for the festivities of life, or at the market place, where the remaining meat was sent and sold. Because of the Corinthian's unusual circumstances, Paul uses wisdom and truth as the basis for his answer to their question. In verse 4, Paul brings us back to his original topic with verses 4-6 giving the theological reason for the Corinthian's freedom to eat meat sacrificed to idols. Let's look at his basic theology here:

2. What 2 things did they collectively *know*, according to verse 4?

    a. Deuteronomy 6:4 gives the mantra of the Jews concerning their one God. What is it?

    b. What is an idol? (You may use your dictionary for help.)

    c. Because someone says that a piece of wood or stone is a *god*, does that make it one? How do we know an idol is *nothing* (verse 4 gives the best answer for this question!)?

Paul makes the concession that there were other so-called *gods* (with a little *g*)—mythological deities and lords worshipped by the cults, and even emperors of that time who were beginning to consider themselves divine and demand worship. But, although the world had gods of their own, there was only one true God—the one who had the ability to save the Corinthians from eternal death and hell.

3. In verse 6, Paul describes the one God the Corinthians had come to believe in.

    ✤ What does he say about *God the Father*?

    ✤ What he say about *the Lord Jesus Christ*?

    a. Paul is using this description of God to help the Corinthians make the contrast between the *real God* they have come to believe in and the *idols* worshipped in Corinth by non-believers. From the content of today's passage (verses 4-6) what is the difference?

Making It Personal

4. As you consider the question that Paul is attempting to answer here, what are your personal thoughts? If there is only one *real God* and idols are really *nothing*, in your own mind, was it all right for the Corinthians to eat meat that had been sacrificed to idols?

Digging Deeper

✤ Isaiah 44:9-20 gives God's description of idols. Read the following verses and answer the questions:

verses 14-17—*What is an idol?*

verses 18-19—*Describe an idol worshipper.*

verse 20—*What is the fruit of idol worship?*

✤ Do your best to summarize today's passage in a couple of sentences.

Day 3
Read 1 Corinthians 8:7-13

Even though the question of the hour was whether it was all right for the Christian Corinthians to eat meat sacrificed to idols, we will see today that Paul made it about something else altogether. To Paul, the question was more about *loving the brethren* than what a believer may or may not eat.

1.   Look at these verses and fill in the blanks:

verse 1—We know_____.
verse 4—We know_____.
verse 7—However_____.

The NIV translates verse 7 simply, "But not everyone knows this," and that is the key. While Paul knew this and while many of the *stronger* Corinthians knew this, everyone did not know that idols were nothing.

a.   How does Paul describe the one who *does not know this,* in verse 7?

We must remember the situation of the Corinthians at this time. They had only recently come out of a lifestyle of idol worship. Although some of these new Christians were able to recognize the truth of the matter, many still associated the meat with the sacrifice and were unable to separate the two. The NASB says it this way, "but some, being accustomed to the idol until now, eat food as if it were sacrificed to an idol." They were accustomed to the fact that meat was offered to idols, and felt that they were defiled if they touched that meat.

2. According to Paul, it doesn't really matter whether you eat or you don't eat, because food does not commend us to God. From verses 9-12, explain what does matter to Paul.

   a. What did Jesus say about stumbling blocks? Matthew 18:7

3. Although Paul had a *strong* conscience, and had a clear understanding of the truth of the matter, to what conclusion did he come? v. 13

Making It Personal
There are many gray areas in life, things that are not specifically addressed in Scripture, like drinking alcohol, playing cards, watching adult movies, and you can probably think of more ...

4. What are some things that you know you cannot touch without being personally defiled? What does Romans 14:23 say about this?

   a. Is there anything others deem wrong, but you feel you can do without sinning? Do you flaunt your liberty? What have you learned in this chapter about stumbling others?

   b. How does *holiness* fit into this subject for you?

Digging Deeper
✚ Tie this week's memory verse (Galatians 5:13) with the heart of what Paul is saying in this chapter.

Day 4
Overview of 1 Corinthians 8

Today we will be looking at the passage we have studied this week as a whole. The goal is to find the main lessons the Lord has for us from this chapter. Don't worry about being clever or profound—just do your best!

Find the Facts ...

1. See if you can state the <u>content</u> of this week's passage in a couple of sentences. You can use your daily summary statements to help you come up with one main theme or summary of the chapter. (Who is speaking, what is taking place, what is the main subject?)

Look for the Heart ...

2. What do you think is the main <u>lesson</u> of this chapter? (What spiritual truths are taught here? Look for a command, a word of exhortation, a promise, etc.)

Hear Him Speak ...

3. Look for a <u>personal application</u> from the content of this chapter. It should come from the lesson you got from the chapter (question 2). How will you apply the lesson to yourself?

4. Was there a particular verse that ministered to you this week? What was it and how did it minister to you?

5. Write out your memory verse *from memory*!

NOTES

FIRST CORINTHIANS: *THE WISDOM OF GOD*
LESSON 10
1 CORINTHIANS 9
✦

As you begin to read chapter 9, it looks as if Paul has entirely left the subject matter of chapter 8 behind, but, in fact, he has not. In chapter 9, Paul uses his own life and choices as an illustration of what he has set the stage for in chapter 8 and will continue with in chapter 10. Paul begins with the question, "Am I not free?" Paul was free indeed! This chapter will give evidence of this fact in a very real and instructive way. *We would do well to make it our aim to live in the freedom that Paul had!*

Day 1
Read 1 Corinthians 9:1-14

1. Using the form of rhetorical questions (some 16 in all), Paul begins by making his claim to be free. What other claims does he make in verse 1?

It seems that there was a dispute among some Corinthians as to whether Paul was truly an apostle or not. Possibly it was those who were *of Apollos*, or *of Cephas* who were questioning this fact.

   a. From verses 1-2, how do the Corinthians themselves prove his apostleship?

   b. What does 2 Corinthians 3:2 say about this?

Paul is not only free and his apostleship proven by their very salvation, but as an apostle, he has certain *rights* that he may lay claim to.

2. What rights does Paul have? (Notice that Paul includes Barnabas in his consideration.)

    verse 4

    verse 5

    verse 6

3. Verses 7-14 give the reasons that Paul may lay claim to these rights, in particular, the right to be paid for his ministry to them:

    ✤ From verse 7, what was simply *common practice*?

    ✤ From verses 8-11, what was *the law* and what could be deduced from it?

    ✤ From verse 13, what was *Jewish custom*?

    ✤ From verse 14, what was *Christ's command*? (See Matthew 10:10b)

Making It Personal

4. What are your thoughts on tithing? We know that tithing is a principle set up in Scripture, but how does today's passage help you to see the importance of sharing materially with those who have shared spiritually with you (see verse 11)?

    a. Are there any changes you need to make in this area—either in a practical way, or maybe just an attitude adjustment? How does Malachi 3:10 encourage you in this area?

Digging Deeper

The word apostle comes from the Greek word *aposotlos* which means to send. It designates the office as instituted by Christ to witness of Him before the world. It also designates the authority which those called to this office possess (from The Complete Word Study Dictionary, Edited by Spiros Zodhiates Th.D.).

The following conditions were the criteria for true apostleship. Note how Paul's experience qualified him as such:

✤ *Witness of the risen Christ—see Acts 1:21-22*

    Paul's experience—

    Acts 9:1-9

    1 Corinthians 9:1

    1 Corinthians 15:7-8

✤ *Commission from Jesus Christ—see Acts 10:39-43; Matthew 28:18-20*

    Paul's experience—

    Acts 9:10-16

✤ *Signs, wonders, and mighty acts—see 2 Corinthians 12:12; Hebrews 2:3-4*

    Paul's experience—

    Acts 13:9-12

✤ Do your best to summarize today's passage in a couple of sentences.

Memory Verse
"We endure all things, that we may cause no hindrance to the gospel of Christ." 1 Corinthians 9:12b

Day 2
Read 1 Corinthians 9:15-23

The verses before us are proof of Paul's great love for mankind, his heart for ministry, and the reality of his personal freedom. In the first 14 verses of chapter 9, Paul gives evidence of his right to receive support from the Corinthian church. In the verses we study today, he waives those rights.

1. Looking back to verse 12, why did Paul waive his rights for support?

a. What was Paul's real reason for preaching the gospel? v. 16

Verse 17 is difficult to understand. Paul did preach voluntarily, and there would indeed be reward for his labor, but, whether voluntarily or not, Paul had been entrusted with a stewardship. He was a man acting under orders!

2. Is there any ministry that you, like Paul, do *of necessity*? Fill in the following blank space: "Woe is me if I do not _____

_____.

Oswald Chambers says of Paul that once he had realized the call of God, there was no competitor for his strength.

a. What *good things* are you giving your strength to? Is there any area that comes to mind that you could *limit* in order to give more to the ministry which *compels you*?

b. What does Paul consider his *reward* for preaching? v. 18

One of the most inspiring passages of Scripture is found in verses 19-23. Paul begins this chapter with the question, "Am I not free?" Verse 19 answers the question—*yes, Paul is free!*

3. Although Paul is truly free, what does he willingly make himself for the sake of mankind? v. 19

a. The reality of Paul's freedom is clearly seen in the subsequent verses. What was Paul free to be:

✤ To the Jews? v. 20   Why?

✤ To the Gentiles? v. 21   Why?

✤ To the weak? v. 22   Why?

✤ To all men? V. 22b   Why?

b. Would Paul have gone against his own conscience in order to become all things to all men? What do you think he means in these verses?

c. How do you see Paul's freedom and maturity in being able to adapt himself to individuals in order to bring them to Christ?

Making It Personal

Paul wasn't legalistic. He was a mature enough Christian to be adaptable. His goal was always bringing others to Christ.

4. In talking to others about Jesus, are you able to adapt to them? Is there anything that you might need to *soften* in order to be a more effective witness for the gospel?

Digging Deeper

The following are examples of Paul freely adapting himself for the sake of ministry. See if you can understand how he did this from these examples. Share what you see.

✜ *To those under the law—*

Acts 16:1-3

Acts 18:18

Acts 21:20-26

✜ *To those not under the law—*

Galatians 2:1-3

Paul only adapted himself when it didn't conflict with what he believed to be a matter of truth and righteousness. Because of this, he was also free to point out a compromise of truth when he witnessed it. Share from the example that follows:

✤ *To Peter when he was acting the hypocrite—*

Galatians 2:11-14

✤ Do your best to summarize today's passage in a couple of sentences.

Day 3
Read 1 Corinthians 9:24-27

Paul's thoughts now turn from personal illustration to a word of exhortation—and what a wonderful exhortation it is! We will be helped in our effort to get ahead spiritually if we can catch the vision of these words!

1. What analogy does Paul use to encourage the Corinthians in their Christian effort?

Even in using this particular analogy as an exhortation to the Corinthians, Paul was adapting himself to them! They would be well acquainted with the analogy of runners running to receive a prize, as the Isthmian games (second only to the Olympics) were held every two years in Corinth. They were eyewitnesses to the training and self-denial involved as athletes readied themselves for the competition.

2, In a typical running race, how many people are able to win?

   a. Is this true of the *Christian* race? (Consider this not as a race for *salvation* but a race for the *rewards of faithful service*.) Still, how does Paul exhort *each* Christian to run? v. 24

3. What are some of the things a runner might do to train for the biggest race of his career? (Would he give his strength to anything else?)

   a. What are some things the runner of the Christian race might do to *run in such a way as to win*? (Consider any similarities to the training of an athletic runner.)

b. What is the difference in the prizes of these two runners?

4. From verse 26 (NASB best), finish these sentences with Paul's example:

*"I run in such a way*_____*."*

*"I box in such a way*_____*."*

a. What kind of *discipline* is Paul referring to when he says, "I discipline my body and bring it into subjection"?

b. When Paul spoke of being *disqualified*, do you think he meant that he would lose his salvation? What do you think he meant?

Making It Personal
5. Paul says that he runs in such a way, as not without aim. Right now (today) in your everyday life, what are you aiming at? Considering your Christian "run," would you say that you are *running in such a way that you may win*? Share honestly.

Digging Deeper
✣ Do your best to summarize today's passage in a couple of sentences.

Day 4
Overview of 1 Corinthians 9
Today we will be looking at the passage we have studied this week as a whole. The goal is to find the main lessons the Lord has for us from this chapter. Don't worry about being clever or profound—just do your best!

Find the Facts ...
1. See if you can state the <u>content</u> of this week's passage in a couple of sentences. You can use your daily summary statements to help you come up with one main theme or summary of the chapter. (Who is speaking, what is taking place, what is the main subject?)

Look for the Heart ...
2. What do you think is the main <u>lesson</u> of this chapter? (What spiritual truths are taught here? Look for a command, a word of exhortation, a promise, etc.)

Hear Him Speak ...
3. Look for a <u>personal application</u> from the content of this chapter. It should come from the lesson you got from the chapter (question 2). How will you apply the lesson to yourself?

4. Was there a particular verse that ministered to you this week? What was it and how did it minister to you?

5. Write out your memory verse *from memory*!

NOTES

FIRST CORINTHIANS: *THE WISDOM OF GOD*
LESSON 11
1 CORINTHIANS 10:1-13
⚜

Paul ends chapter 9 with the words, "But I discipline my body and bring it into subjection, lest, when I have preached to others, I myself should become disqualified" (NKJV). In chapter 10, he begins by using the nation of Israel as an illustration of some who *were* disqualified. This chapter speaks to us of self-discipline.

Day 1
Read 1 Corinthians 10:1-5

1. Who does Paul use as an example to the Corinthians of those who were not *self-disciplined* (what does he call them)? v. 1

   a. From the context of this passage, share who these people actually were. (You may see Exodus 12:51 for help.)

   b. Were these the Corinthians' actual (physical) fathers? How were they related to the Corinthians?

2. Paul uses the word *all* five times in this passage, pointing out the spiritual advantages that *all* their fathers had. Look at these verses and share your understanding of the special privileges these Israelites had:

   ⚜ *all were under the cloud*—Exodus 13:21-22; 14:19

   ⚜ *all passed through the sea*—Exodus 14:21-29

✤ *all were baptized into Moses*—This concept is a little difficult. The word here for baptized, *baptizo*, in its more general implications means *to be identified*. With that thought in mind, see if you can define what Paul might have meant here. Use Galatians 3:27 for help.

✤ *all ate the same spiritual food*—Exodus 16:12-15, 35

✤ *all drank the same spiritual drink*—Exodus 17:1-7; Numbers 20:1-11

3. In contrast to the spiritual privileges given *all* of Israel, as they were led out of Egypt by the mercy and grace of God, verse 5 offers a sad conclusion. What was the outcome for *most* of them?

Making It Personal
4. If you are a believer in Christ, you are part of the *privileged group* that has received *every spiritual blessing in Christ Jesus* (Ephesians 1:3). You are one of the *privileged group* that has been given *all things that pertain to life and godliness,* through the knowledge of Jesus (2 Peter 1:3). Consider yourself as one who lives a *privileged life,* being led, fed, and continually blessed by the Holy Spirit of God. How does this make you feel? Are you thankful for these great privileges? Do you even realize you have them? Share your thoughts.

a. What warning do verses 1-5 give *you* (share from your heart)?

Digging Deeper
"… And all ate the same spiritual food; and all drank the same spiritual drink; for they were drinking from a spiritual rock which followed them; and that rock was Christ." It seems that Jewish legend held that a real (material) rock actually followed the Israelites on their wilderness journey. Paul shows us that it was Christ who was with them all the time!

✤ How do these verses reveal Christ as our provision of spiritual food and spiritual drink? John 6:31-35, 48-58; John 7:37

✤ Do your best to summarize today's passage in a couple of sentences.

Memory Verse
"Therefore, let him who thinks he stands take heed lest he fall." 1 Corinthians 10:12

Day 2
Read 1 Corinthians 10:6-10

This portion of Scripture tells us *why* the Israelites fell in the wilderness. Harvard philosophy professor George Santayana made the profound point that, "Those who cannot remember the past are condemned to repeat it."

1. Share from the following verses the account of Israel's sin and God's wrath in each case mentioned by Paul. (Share in your own words your understanding of what happened.) *Now these things happened as examples for us, that we should not …*

   ✤ *crave evil things, as they also craved*—Numbers 11:4-6, 31-34

   ✤ *be idolaters, as some of them were*—Exodus 32:1-6, 28

   ✤ *act immorally, as some of them did*—Numbers 25:1-9

Paul speaks here of one day, probably the first day of judgment, when 23,000 fell. Numbers records *all* who died by the plague, 24,000.

   ✤ *try the Lord, as some of them did*—Numbers 21:4-6

   ✤ *grumble, as some of them did*—Numbers 16:1-3, 16-35

Making It Personal

Consider the sins of Israel that kept *most* of them from entering the Promised Land: lusting after something they did not have, idol worship, sexual immorality, tempting the Lord with complaints, murmuring against God and His leaders. Is there an area here in which you struggle? Ask God today to help you in that area. Commit this area and yourself to Him. Trust Him that what He has given you is what you need (including Himself and the leaders He has placed over you), or He would have given you something else! Take this seriously! 1 Corinthians 11:31 says, "For if we would judge ourselves, we would not be judged."

Digging Deeper

✝ Because of the sins mentioned in our passage today, *most* of the Israelites didn't enter the Promised Land, even Moses was denied the privilege. In fact, all but two of the adults that left Egypt died in the wilderness. When we are truly saved, we know that we can't lose our salvation (see Romans 5:8-10; Ephesians 1:5, 13-14), but consider the point of *not being allowed entrance into the land of promise.* What might this mean to you in regard to your spiritual journey here on earth?

✝ Do your best to summarize today's passage in a couple of sentences.

Day 3
Read 1 Corinthians 10:11-13

1. Why does verse 11 tell us these things happened and were recorded for us?

One of the meanings of this word "example" is *type.* Israel's experiences were *typical* experiences. H.A. Ironside, in his commentary on 1 Corinthians, says, "These incidents took place literally just as we are told they did, but their significance was something beyond their place in history." God knew, if His people were wise, they would take the events of the past and learn from them. God wastes nothing!

2. Considering what we have studied in this portion of Scripture, which began in chapter 8 with Paul answering a question about meat sacrificed to idols, who do you think he might be addressing in verse 12? See 1 Corinthians 8:1-3, 9.

   a. The Israelites were *spiritually blessed* by God in their wilderness journey, and yet *most* of them fell to temptation. What is Paul's point to the *spiritually enriched* and *highly blessed* Corinthians, in verse 12?

b. How can you apply this admonition to yourself today?

3. Although the temptation to sin is always there and falling to temptation is always possible, verse 13 encourages us that we need not fall! Break down verse 13 by answering the following questions:

✤ Is the thing that tempts you today unique?

✤ Who is in control of the degree of your particular temptation? Can He be trusted?

✤ What will always be provided so that you will be able to endure?

✤ How does this verse assure you *personally* that no temptation to sin or trial of your faith need ever cause you to sin?

Making It Personal
4. Read Hebrews 10:36-39 and apply these words to the thing you are being tempted or tested in today.

Digging Deeper
✤ Tie this week's memory verse (1 Corinthians 10:12) with the heart of what Paul is saying in this chapter.

Day 4
Overview of 1 Corinthians 10:1-13
Today we will be looking at the passage we have studied this week as a whole. The goal is to find the main lessons the Lord has for us from this chapter. Don't worry about being clever or profound—just do your best!

Find the Facts ...
1. See if you can state the <u>content</u> of this week's passage in a couple of sentences. You can use your daily summary statements to help you come up with one main theme or summary of the chapter. (Who is speaking, what is taking place, what is the main subject?)

Look for the Heart ...

2. What do you think is the main <u>lesson</u> of this chapter? (What spiritual truths are taught here? Look for a command, a word of exhortation, a promise, etc.)

Hear Him Speak ...

3. Look for a <u>personal application</u> from the content of this chapter. It should come from the lesson you got from the chapter (question 2). How will you apply the lesson to yourself?

4. Was there a particular verse that ministered to you this week? What was it and how did it minister to you?

5. Write out your memory verse *from memory*!

NOTES

FIRST CORINTHIANS: *THE WISDOM OF GOD*
LESSON 12
1 CORINTHIANS 10:14-33
⚜

Beginning in chapter 8, Paul has been responding to a question about eating meat sacrificed to idols. Although he will get back to that point in our verses today, he begins by giving a strong word of warning to the Corinthian church.

Day 1
Read 1 Corinthians 10:14-22

1. What was Paul's exhortation to the Corinthians? v. 14

Notice how he addresses his readers with the words, *my beloved*. His strong exhortation to them on this point is a revelation of his true love for them.

a. What does the word flee mean?

The Amplified Bible amplifies the word *flee* this way: keep clear away from, avoid by flight if need be.

b. What exactly is idolatry?

c. From what we have studied so far about Corinth, why would Paul need to exhort them so strongly in this matter?

Because this is a difficult passage, in the remainder of this day's study we will be a *digging deeper*!

Digging Deeper

2. Paul uses the imagery of the Lord's Supper to help them get the true spiritual impact of what it is to worship an idol. In the NASB, Paul speaks of us having *a sharing* in the cup and the bread. The NKJV uses the word *communion*, and the NIV uses *participate*. The Greek word is *koinonia*, which speaks of partnership, participation, and fellowship. Answer these questions from verses 16-17:

   a. Explain what we are participating in when we drink the cup of Communion. (What does this cup represent?)

   b. Explain what we are participating in when we partake of the bread of Communion. (What does this bread represent?)

   c. How is it that in sharing Communion we are sharing in the sacrifice of Christ?

   d. How is it that in sharing Communion we become one with those who partake with us?

   e. How was this same concept true of the Israelites who made sacrifices for their sin? v. 18

3. Is an idol itself anything? What does the sacrifice to the idol represent?

   a. What is Paul's point?

Making It Personal

4. Read 2 Corinthians 6:14-18 and answer the following:

   a. Why is it important that a Christian take a stand of *no compromise* with the world?

   b. Have you taken this stand? See verse 17.

c. What is the promise? v. 18 How does this speak to you personally?

Digging Deeper

1 Corinthians 10:22 speaks of *provoking the Lord to jealousy*. Exodus 34:14 says. "... for you shall not worship any other god, for the Lord, whose name is Jealous, is a jealous God ..." Do your best to summarize today's passage in a couple of sentences, from the standpoint of the jealousy of God over *you*, His beloved.

Memory Verse

"Whether, then, you eat or drink or whatever you do, do all to the glory of God." 1 Corinthians 10:31

Day 2

Read 1 Corinthians 10:23-30

In saying all things are *lawful* (legitimate, permissible), Paul is speaking of those areas that we call "gray areas," those things not specifically forbidden by Scripture. Throughout the rest of this chapter, several rules are given by which we may govern our decisions in those gray areas of life.

1. When something is Scripturally permissible, what is the rule in assessing whether or not it should be done?

    ✣ verse 23a

    ✣ verse 23b

    ✣ verse 24

    a. How did the beginning of Paul's thoughts on this subject strike this same chord? (See 1 Corinthians 8:1, and consider again the meaning of the word *edify*.)

2. What is Paul's specific word on the subject of eating what is sold in the meat market? v. 25

    a. What is his reasoning on this? v. 26 (Explain what he is saying.)

3.   What is Paul's specific word for the occasion of eating at the home of an unbeliever? v. 27

a.   What if it is announced that the meat was offered in sacrifice? vv. 28-29

b.   Why was Paul not concerned with his own conscience? (See vv. 29-30 with v. 26 and 1 Cor. 8:4 in mind.)

Making It Personal
The Amplified Bible translates verse 24 this way: "Let no one then seek his own good and advantage and profit, but [rather] each one of the other [let him seek the welfare of his neighbor]."

4.   Is there an area in your life right now in which you might be able to apply Paul's words (perhaps in your marriage or in a relationship with a parent, child, or friend)? This is not always easy for us to do, but stopping and realizing that we might *need* to do this is a start! How might you begin to seek the welfare of this one the Lord has laid on your heart?

Digging Deeper
✣ Summarize today's passage, considering verses 28-29 in the light of verses 23-24.

Day 3
Read 1 Corinthians 10:31-33

1.   Paul gives two more *rules of thumb* in these final verses of chapter 10:

✣ verse 31

✣ verse 32

2.   What was Paul's habit, according to verse 33?

   a. How do Paul's words here, again, line up with verse 24?

   b. Was Paul a people-pleaser? What was his purpose in pleasing *all men in all things?*

   c. How did he say this most beautifully in 1 Corinthians 9:19?

3. Although chapter 10 ends with verse 33, it is thought by many that the first verse of chapter 11 actually finishes Paul's thoughts here. If this is true, what is the final exhortation of this passage?

   a. What, specifically, is Paul encouraging them (and us) to do? (Consider what he has taught in our passage today.)

Making It Personal

In these chapters, Paul has let us know that he was at liberty. John says, "Therefore if the Son makes you free, you shall be free indeed" (John 8:36 NKJV). Paul was indeed a free man! But his goal was to glorify God (verse 31) and to bring others to salvation (verse 33), even at the expense of his own liberty.

4. Is there any area in your life in which you are not at liberty? Share your thoughts here. Won't you begin today to bring that area to the Lord and ask Him to give you victory there?

   a. Is there any area of your life in which you realize that you aren't bringing glory to God? What steps can you take to begin to change that fact?

Digging Deeper

✤ Tie this week's memory verse (1 Corinthians 10:31) with the heart of what Paul is saying in this chapter.

Day 4
Overview of 1 Corinthians 10:14-33

Today we will be looking at the passage we have studied this week as a whole. The goal is to find the main lessons the Lord has for us from this chapter. Don't worry about being clever or profound—just do your best!

Find the Facts ...

1. See if you can state the <u>content</u> of this week's passage in a couple of sentences. You can use your daily summary statements to help you come up with one main theme or summary of the chapter. (Who is speaking, what is taking place, what is the main subject?)

Look for the Heart ...

2. What do you think is the main <u>lesson</u> of this chapter? (What spiritual truths are taught here? Look for a command, a word of exhortation, a promise, etc.)

Hear Him Speak ...

3. Look for a <u>personal application</u> from the content of this chapter. It should come from the lesson you got from the chapter (question 2). How will you apply the lesson to yourself?

4. Was there a particular verse that ministered to you this week? What was it and how did it minister to you?

5. Write out your memory verse *from memory*!

NOTES

FIRST CORINTHIANS: *THE WISDOM OF GOD*
LESSON 13
1 CORINTHIANS 11

❧

Paul now moves on to another topic in his letter to the Corinthians. In chapter 11, he begins to deal with the Corinthians' behavior during public worship, beginning with the question of head coverings. He will also address their behavior during the Lord's Supper and, in chapters 12-14, the use of spiritual gifts. Remember, as you study these chapters, that the motivation of Paul is to see to it that they are respecting one another and the Lord during worship.

Day 1
Read 1 Corinthians 11:1-16

As was stated in our last lesson, verse 1 most likely belongs as a final thought with the message of chapter 10. But, if we look at verse 1 as belonging in chapter 11, we again see Paul encouraging them to imitate him (verse 1) and then praising them for following the teachings he has given them (verse 2). Paul uses the method of first handing them the bouquet, before dropping the bomb. The bomb begins to drop in verse 3, with the words, "But I want you to understand …"

1.   What does Paul want them to understand? v. 3

The word for head here is *kephale* which means the head, top, or that which is uppermost in relation to something. It speaks, in regard to people, of the chief or one in authority. Although we can look at this verse as speaking of one being in authority and another in subordination, Paul only mentions the one who is the head, never designating the position of the other. From the rest of Paul's thoughts on the subject, it may be that Paul's emphasis is on *the honor due to the one who is the head.*

a.   How important do you think this piece of information is, not only for the Corinthians, but for us as Christians today?

2. From our passage today, what is Paul's specific word to the man on:

   ✤ *The covering of his head?*

   ✤ *His hair length? (v. 14)*

   a. Who would the man disgrace if he didn't follow Paul's instructions in this area? v. 4

   b. Who exactly is this? v. 3

3. From our passage today, what is Paul's specific word to the woman on:

   ✤ *The covering of her head?*

   ✤ *Her hair length? (v. 15)*

   a. Who would the woman disgrace if she didn't follow Paul's instructions in this area? v. 5

   b. Who exactly is this? v.3

Making It Personal

4. If you are married, what do you think the significance is to you that your husband is your head?

   a. How might you show your husband honor—especially in the context of the public worship (church) experience?

5. If you are not married, who do you think your head would be?

a. Is there a way in which you can show your head more honor—especially in the context of public worship?

Digging Deeper

In this passage, Paul gives the picture both of subordination and equality when speaking of the *man* and the *woman*, (which can also be translated *husband* and *wife*).

✤ How do verses 8-9 show the reason for the subordination of the woman to the man?

✤ How do verses 11-12 show the reason for the equality of men and women.

✤ See if you can take both of these truths and come to a conclusion about the position of men and women in relation to one another.

✤ Do your best to summarize today's passage in a couple of sentences.

Memory Verse

"Be subject to one another in the fear of Christ." Ephesians 5:21

Day 2
Read 1 Corinthians 11:17-26

Paul began this chapter by praising the Corinthians (verse 2). At this turn in the letter, though, he says, "But in giving this instruction, I do not praise you …" Here he begins his teaching on the behavior of the church during the Lord's Supper, behavior which was completely unfitting for the worship service in general but even more for the ceremony remembering and honoring the Lord's sacrifice.

Paul has *heard* that there were divisions among the Corinthians in regard to their celebration of the Lord's Supper. The divisions he speaks of here are not the same divisions he spoke of in the beginning of this letter, but divisions within the body between those who were rich and those who were poor.

To help with our understanding of the situation, we need to know that in the early days of the church there would be a love feast held prior to the celebration of the Lord's Supper. It was here that the problem had begun. Reading this passage in the NLT could be helpful to your understanding.

1. From verses 20-22, see if you can get an understanding of the specifics of the problem. Share what you understand.

    a. Can you see how this would cause divisions between those *with* and those *without*?

2. See if you can apply the teachings of James 2:1-6a to Paul's concern here.

    a. What is the law we are to live by? James 2:8 Whose law is this? (See Matthew 22:37-39.)

    b. What would Jesus have thought about this situation? (Especially in regard to the very thing they were celebrating—His *sacrifice* for them.)

3. In verses 23-26, Paul gives the Corinthians a reminder of what he had received as to the original expression of the Lord's Supper. Answer these questions for an understanding of the significance of this event.

verse 23
   ✣ *When* did the original Lord's Supper take place?

   ✣ *What* was the first element to be taken?

verse 24
   ✣ What did Jesus do with this element?

   ✣ What did this signify?

verse 25

✤ What was the second element to be taken?

✤ What did Jesus say was the significance of this element?

verse 26

✤ What was the partaking of these elements to signify for the body of Christ?

a. Share from these thoughts (actually *facts*) why Paul would be so distraught over the behavior of the Corinthians in celebrating this important Christian rite.

Making It Personal

4. What is your heart during the Communion service? Do you realize the significance of what is taking place? Do you really *remember* Jesus at this time, considering what He has done for you, or do you find your thoughts wandering, thinking of what you need to do later? Determine in your heart that the next time you partake in this holy observance, you will do so with a heart and mind that is captivated by the truth of what it represents: Jesus hung on *your* cross.

Digging Deeper

✤ Compare these passages on the Lord's Supper with our passage today, and see if you find anything that adds to your understanding of this most precious moment: Matthew 26:26-29; Luke 22:14-20

✤ Do your best to summarize today's passage in a couple of sentences.

Day 3
Read 1 Corinthians 11:27-34

After sharing the deep meaning of the Communion service, Paul now shares the consequences of partaking in an *unworthy manner*.

1. Name some ways a person might partake of Communion in an unworthy manner.

a. What is the one who partakes unworthily guilty of, according to verse 27?

This is a difficult concept. The Life Application Bible Commentary on 1 and 2 Corinthians explains it this way: "To treat the symbols of Christ's ultimate sacrifice irreverently is to be guilty of irreverence toward His body and blood shed on sinners' behalf. Instead of honoring Christ's sacrifice, those who ate unworthily were sharing in the guilt of those who crucified Him."

2. What is Paul's suggestion prior to the taking of the Communion? v. 28

We most often apply this verse to the fact that an *unbeliever* is not to partake of this "family" observance, as he would obviously be profaning the precious blood that he doesn't even believe in! This is an accurate application. We also apply this to the fact that each individual believer should look within and consider if they are coming to the Communion table with known sin in their lives. Of course, repentance is the step that must be taken in order to be prepared to partake. This is also an important aspect. But, thinking in terms of the context of this passage so far and what Paul is trying to communicate to them here, we must also consider the aspect of loving our neighbor and caring for the welfare of those who are not as well off as ourselves.

a. Does Paul say of the one who examines himself that he should *not* partake? What is Paul's hope in this matter? v. 28

3. What happens to the one who partakes unworthily? v. 29

a. What was the result of this very sin right there in the midst of the Corinthian church? v. 30

4. What is Paul's simple answer according to verse 31?

a. If we don't judge ourselves, what will be the result? v. 32

b. What is God's purpose in this discipline? (see v. 30 with v. 32 and share what you believe he is saying.)

c.   What is Paul's final analysis of this subject?

verse 33

verse 34

Making It Personal

5.   Share any new appreciation you have for the sacrifice Jesus made on your behalf; any new appreciation you have for the ritual we share in the Lord's Supper; or any new appreciation you have about your personal responsibility in partaking of it.

Digging Deeper

✣ Tie this week's memory verse (Ephesians 5:21) with the heart of what Paul is saying in this chapter as a whole.

Day 4
Overview of 1 Corinthians 11

Today we will be looking at the passage we have studied this week as a whole. The goal is to find the main lessons the Lord has for us from this chapter. Don't worry about being clever or profound—just do your best!

Find the Facts …

1.   See if you can state the content of this week's passage in a couple of sentences. You can use your daily summary statements to help you come up with one main theme or summary of the chapter. (Who is speaking, what is taking place, what is the main subject?)

Look for the Heart …

2.   What do you think is the main lesson of this chapter? (What spiritual truths are taught here? Look for a command, a word of exhortation, a promise, etc.)

Hear Him Speak ...

3. Look for a <u>personal application</u> from the content of this chapter. It should come from the lesson you got from the chapter (question 2). How will you apply the lesson to yourself?

4. Was there a particular verse that ministered to you this week? What was it and how did it minister to you?

5. Write out your memory verse *from memory*!

NOTES

FIRST CORINTHIANS: *THE WISDOM OF GOD*
LESSON 14
1 CORINTHIANS 12:1-13

Continuing with the theme of behavior in public worship, Paul now responds to another question brought by the Corinthians. The words, "Now concerning," reveal that he is moving in a new direction, responding to specific questions or issues that have been raised. The concern of chapters 12-14 is the matter of spiritual gifts.

Where verse 1 has translated *spiritual gifts*, the actual wording in the Greek is *pneumatikos*, which simply means spiritual. It may refer to spiritual things, spiritual matters, or spiritual persons. The word for gift, *charisma*, is not actually introduced until verse 4. We might translate verse 1, "Now concerning spiritual things" or "Now concerning matters of the spirit" (or perhaps even "matters of the Spirit").

Day 1
Read 1 Corinthians 12:1-3

1. What is Paul's desire for the Corinthians, in bringing up the subject of *spiritual things*? v. 1

We realize that they have asked some specific questions on this subject, but there is also evidence in this chapter and chapter 14 that there was some misunderstanding in this church concerning the purpose and work of the gifts. These chapters form a sort of apologetic for the true nature and purpose of spiritual gifts. It seems the Corinthians were equating spirituality with the more spectacular and outward gifts. This was causing rivalries in the congregation, as well as jealousy and chaos in worship. Paul wants to help them see the truth.

2. In their former pagan religious ceremonies, where were they led? v. 2

    a. Who was influencing them as they were led astray?

The fact that these idols were *dumb* means that they were voiceless or could not communicate. Evidently they "spoke" through their worshippers in what was called *ecstatic* or *inspired* speech. This could easily be confused with the spiritual gift of tongues, which was a genuine manifestation of the Holy Spirit through believers in Christ. Others may have been giving forth prophecy or what they were calling a word of knowledge or wisdom. Paul gives them the formula so that they might know whether or not a word is inspired by the Holy Spirit of God.

3. If the speaker (of religious things) is *not* speaking by the power of the Holy Spirit, how would this eventually be known?

    a. If the speaker *is* speaking by the power of the Holy Spirit, what will be the heart and result of their message?

4. Does your *mouth* say Jesus is Lord? What does Romans 10:9-10 say about this?

    a. Does your *life* say Jesus is Lord? Is there any area in your life that gives lie to the fact that this is your testimony? What can you do about this?

Making It Personal
If you read a book or hear a message that has good things to say, even things that you recognize as true, but does not lead you to recognize your need for Jesus as Lord and Savior, no matter how many good things it tells you, is it truly good?

5. What should you recognize about philosophical books or self-help messages that never lead you to Christ? Have you had an experience with this? Share your experience and what you learned.

Digging Deeper
✝ Do your best to summarize today's passage in a couple of sentences.

Memory Verse
"A spiritual gift is given to each of us as a means of helping the entire church." 1 Corinthians 12:7 NLT

Day 2
Read 1 Corinthians 12:4-7

A main theme of chapter 12 is *unity in diversity*. That theme begins to shine forth in the verses we study today.

1. How do you see *diversity* in verses 4-6?

The word diversities in verse 4 is the Greek word *diairesis* which means difference, distinction, variety.

    a. Is there only one gift? Name some of the varieties of spiritual gifts. (You may see verses 8-10 for help.)

    b. Is there only one ministry? Name some of the different types of ministry. (You may see verse 28 for help.)

The word for activities is *energima* which means operations, workings, effects. It could be defined as *different ways God works.* Verse 7 NLT says "There are different ways God works in our lives, but it is the same God who does the work through all of us." We might consider the fact that the same God works through different people in different ways, even people with the same gift.

    c. What might be some different ways God could use a person with the gift of teaching?

    d. Does this open up to you an understanding of the varieties of gifts, the varieties of ministries, and the varieties of God's activities?

2. What does the teaching of verses 4-6 mean to you?

    a. How would these thoughts help the Corinthians, who may have been singling out particular gifts and people as being more important than others?

3. How do you see *unity* in verses 4-6?

What a beautiful picture of the Triune God as the source and distributor of the gifts of the Spirit. God the Father, Jesus His Son, and the Holy Spirit are in complete control of every aspect of the gifts!

4. For whom are the gifts actually given? v. 7 What does this mean?

    a. How would this fact help turn the Corinthians' thinking around?

Making It Personal
5. Have you found yourself coveting a particular gift of the Spirit? Perhaps you have even been jealous of someone with the gift you want. How does our passage today clarify your thinking on this point?

    a. Have you thought you had no gifts? How does verse 7 dispel this lie of the enemy?

Digging Deeper
✝ Do your best to summarize today's passage in a couple of sentences.

Day 3
Read 1 Corinthians 12:8-13

1. From verses 8-10, name the gifts Paul lists here for the Corinthians. Beside each gift share your understanding of what that gift actually is.

    verse 8

    ✝

    ✝

verse 9

✤

✤

verse 10

✤

✤

✤

✤

✤

2.   Where, again, is the unity found in this diverse list of gifts? v. 11

a.   Can you take any personal pride in the gifts you have been given? What insight does John 15:5 give on this point?

Alan Redpath says, "We have nothing unless we receive it from Him." This thought should forever cancel out any pride and, in fact, should bring deep humility as we seek to exercise the gifts we have been graciously given.

3.   How is the human body a picture of diversity in unity? v. 12

a.   What do you think Paul means when he says, *"all the members of the body, though they are many, are one body, **so also is Christ**"*?

4. In verse 13, Paul speaks of the fact that all believers have been baptized into the body of Christ by the Holy Spirit. How does that truth eliminate race, social status, and even sex? (Also see Galatians 3:28.)

Making It Personal

The Life Application Bible Commentary on 1 and 2 Corinthians makes the point that God's purpose in giving gifts has nothing to do with self-esteem. We are not to seek for or ask for gifts to help us feel important or significant, but instead, by making ourselves available to God and seeking to serve others for His sake, our gifts will come. It offers these steps to help us recognize what our gifts might be:

1) Ask God to increase your usefulness.
2) Seek opportunities of service.
3) Observe how others serve.
4) Ask those you've served and those who serve with you to help you discern your spiritual strengths.
5) Practice those gifts even more.

Digging Deeper

✣ As an overview of this lesson in chapter 12, consider how the Holy Spirit is the *unifier* of the body of Christ.

✣ Tie this week's memory verse (1 Corinthians 12:7) with the heart of what Paul is saying in this chapter as a whole.

Day 4
Overview of 1 Corinthians 12:1-13

Today we will be looking at the passage we have studied this week as a whole. The goal is to find the main lessons the Lord has for us from this chapter. Don't worry about being clever or profound—just do your best!

Find the Facts …

1. See if you can state the <u>content</u> of this week's passage in a couple of sentences. You can use your daily summary statements to help you come up with one main theme or summary of the chapter. (Who is speaking, what is taking place, what is the main subject?)

Look for the Heart ...

2. What do you think is the main <u>lesson</u> of this chapter? (What spiritual truths are taught here? Look for a command, a word of exhortation, a promise, etc.)

Hear Him Speak ...

3. Look for a <u>personal application</u> from the content of this chapter. It should come from the lesson you got from the chapter (question 2). How will you apply the lesson to yourself?

4. Was there a particular verse that ministered to you this week? What was it and how did it minister to you?

5. Write out your memory verse *from memory*!

NOTES

FIRST CORINTHIANS: *THE WISDOM OF GOD*
LESSON 15
1 CORINTHIANS 12:14-31

⚜

The theme of *unity in diversity*, which began in verse 4, continues on in the verses we will study this week, with a small twist: verses 14-19 present *unity in diversity* while verses 20-26 reveal *diversity in unity*, and finally, verses 27-31 underline, once again, God's sovereignty in the appointment of the gifts.

Day 1
Read 1 Corinthians 12:14-19

The *human body* is the illustration Paul uses to help us understand the *spiritual body* of Christ—the Church. It will be helpful for us to try to use our imaginations as we study these verses, to really gain an understanding of the body of Christ, as a whole, and to see the significance that each of us has within that body.

Unity in diversity:

1. We know that we have just one *body*, but to make up our body there are many *members* or we could say *parts*. Make a list of some of the *parts* of which the human body is made up—be *diverse* in your list!

   a. What are some of the *parts* that make up the body of Christ? (We studied some of these in our last lesson, but you can add to that list.)

   b. Do you recognize what your part in this body is? Share with your group your understanding of the gift(s) you've been given and the avenue God has given you to use them.

Paul gives three pictures to help the Corinthians realize the value of their gifts, no matter what they are, especially for those who think their gifts might be insignificant. He uses a foot/hand scenario—the foot thinking it is not important because it isn't a hand; an ear/eye scenario—the ear thinking that it is of no value because it doesn't happen to be an eye; and then he gives us a rather funny image to consider—that of the whole body being an eye!

2. Consider the last scenario Paul uses—that of the whole body being an eye (v. 17): What would life be like for you if you could *see* but not *hear, taste, feel,* or *smell*? What would be lost to you?

3. Now let's apply the truths of verses 15-17 to the gifts of the Spirit:

    a. What would happen to the body of Christ if there were prophets, pastors, and teachers, but no *administrators*? Consider this Bible study; would it be able to function properly with teachers only? What if there were no administrators or no leaders?

    b. Consider your pastor—would he be able to function without those with the gift of *helps*?

    c. Acts 6:2-4 gives us a Scriptural example of just this need. Share from this passage the need and solution of the spiritual leaders of the day.

The Amplified Bible translates verse 15 as a question: "If the foot should say, because I am not a hand, I am not a part of the body, *is it for this reason any less a part of the body?*" The obvious answer is that of course it is still a part of the body—and a very needful one at that!

Making It Personal
4. From verse 18, how exactly did God place the members of the body of Christ?

    a. Do you believe this for yourself? Are you thankful for your gift(s)? Are you thankful for the place God has given you in His body? Do you recognize that no matter what your gift is, it is important to the whole body of Christ? Use verses 15-17 to see the importance of not belittling yourself and your gift(s).

Digging Deeper
✤ Do your best to summarize today's passage in a couple of sentences.

Memory Verse
"But to each one of us grace was given according to the measure of Christ's gift." Ephesians 4:7

Day 2
Read 1 Corinthians 12:20-26

In verses 15-17, Paul addressed one concern, an individual member of the body of Christ considering themselves unimportant to the rest of the body because they perceive their gift to be of lesser value: "Because I am not a hand, I am not a part of the body" (verse 15). In today's passage, he speaks to the member who considers himself superior. This was the greater problem in Corinth, and this is the problem that created Paul's first scenario. How generous of Paul to first address himself to those who were intimidated by the Corinthians who thought their gifts made them superior.

Diversity in unity:
1. Can any one member of the body of Christ truthfully say they don't need another? v. 21

Consider having an eye but no hands. You could see where you were going, but you couldn't do much when you got there! And the head is pretty important, but if it had no feet, it could do nothing but think!

a. What does this tell you about the body of Christ?

2. Speaking of the *human* body, what does Paul tell us about:

✤ *The weaker parts* (v. 22)?

✤ *The less honorable parts* (v. 23)?

✤ *The unpresentable parts* (v. 23)?

✤ Apply one of these analogies to the body of Christ.

3. How has God composed the body, according to verse 24?

   a. Why has He done it this way? v. 25

   b. Verse 25 is truly the heart of what Paul is trying to communicate to the Corinthians—and to us! What is his exhortation here?

Making It Personal

Paul says that when one part of the body suffers, all the parts of the body suffer with it, and when one part of the body is honored, all the parts of the body rejoice. To help us get the picture Paul is painting here, we might consider what happens when we slam our finger in the door—*ouch!*—everything hurts! Or when our mouth receives a bite of our favorite ice cream—*yum!*—the tongue, the taste buds, the throat, and the tummy all get blessed! That is how it is with the human body. Is that how it is in the body of Christ?

4. Romans 12:15 tells us, "Rejoice with those who rejoice, and weep with those who weep." How do you react when a brother or sister in the Lord is suffering? Do you suffer with them? Is there any improvement needed in this area? Do you know someone who is suffering right now? How might you show them empathy?

   a. Sometimes a harder thing is to *rejoice with those who rejoice*. Are you able to rejoice with your brothers and sisters in the Lord when they are celebrating? Is there any improvement needed in this area? Is there someone you know who has just gotten a special blessing—maybe a new home, a new ministry opportunity, a job promotion, etc., with whom you might rejoice?

Digging Deeper

✝ Do your best to summarize today's passage in a couple of sentences.

Day 3
Read 1 Corinthians 12:27-31

Paul says that we are the body of Christ (amazing!), and members individually. In other words, just as our bodies have body parts, we make up those body parts of Christ here on earth! We all have our own individual function to fulfill the work of Christ in this world. We are His arms, legs, feet, and hands! What an honor He has given us! We must be careful to be grateful for the gifts He has sovereignly chosen to bestow upon us.

God's sovereignty in the appointment of gifts:

1. Name the appointments/gifts Paul lists in these verses:

⚜

⚜

⚜

⚜

⚜

⚜

⚜

⚜

2. What is the first appointment Paul mentions?

    a. Share what you know about this gift. (We have looked at this gift previously in our studies this year.)

    b. Do you think there is any significance in the fact that Paul began his list with apostle?

3. What is the last gift Paul mentions?

    a. What do you know about this gift? (You may see Acts 2 for help.)

    b. Can you think of any significance in the fact that Paul named this gift last?

4. What is Paul trying to communicate in verses 29-30?

    a. There is a teaching in our day that says that the gift of tongues always accompanies the baptism of the Holy Spirit (as it did at Pentecost). Or, in other words, if you do not have the gift of tongues, then you aren't baptized in the Holy Spirit. According to this passage, can this teaching be true? What is true?

5. Read Ephesians 4:11. Notice the same theme running through Paul's list of gifts in this verse. How many does he say were apostles, prophets, and evangelists?

    a. Ephesians 4:12 tells us why these offices were given. Why was that?

Making It Personal
In Ephesians 4, when Paul lists some of the gifts Jesus Christ gave the Church, he says it this way: "And He gave some as apostles, and some as prophets, and some as evangelists, and some as pastors and teachers, for the equipping of the saints for the work of service, to the building up of the body of Christ." He doesn't say that he gave some men *these gifts*, but that He gave *them—the gifted men*, to the church. Do you realize that *you*, along with the gifts you've been given, are a gift to the Church? What difference might this truth make in your obedience to God's call?

Digging Deeper
✤ Tie this week's memory verse (Ephesians 4:7) with the heart of what Paul is saying in this chapter as a whole.

Day 4
Overview of 1 Corinthians 12:14-31
Today we will be looking at the passage we have studied this week as a whole. The goal is to find the main lessons the Lord has for us from this chapter. Don't worry about being clever or profound—just do your best!

Find the Facts ...

1. See if you can state the <u>content</u> of this week's passage in a couple of sentences. You can use your daily summary statements to help you come up with one main theme or summary of the chapter. (Who is speaking, what is taking place, what is the main subject?)

Look for the Heart ...

2. What do you think is the main <u>lesson</u> of this chapter? (What spiritual truths are taught here? Look for a command, a word of exhortation, a promise, etc.)

Hear Him Speak ...

3. Look for a <u>personal application</u> from the content of this chapter. It should come from the lesson you got from the chapter (question 2). How will you apply the lesson to yourself?

4. Was there a particular verse that ministered to you this week? What was it and how did it minister to you?

5. Write out your memory verse *from memory*!

NOTES

FIRST CORINTHIANS: *THE WISDOM OF GOD*
LESSON 16
1 CORINTHIANS 13

⚜

1 Corinthians 13 has become known as the *love chapter* of the Bible! In chapter 13, Paul shows us the *more excellent way* he spoke of at the end of chapter 12! In the midst of three chapters on the gifts of the Spirit, Paul lifts up the greatest gift—really not a gift but a grace—and pronounces love to be the highest attainment. Although set in the midst of much rebuke and needful instruction, Alan Redpath says of this chapter, "everything in (it) is fragrant"!

Day 1
Read 1 Corinthians 13:1-3

Paul began chapter 12 with the words, "Now concerning spiritual gifts, brethren, I do not want you to be unaware." Paul had been asked a question about the gifts of the Spirit, and he wanted the believers in Corinth to have a greater understanding of their purpose and value. It is clear from all of Paul's words on the subject that the Corinthians put particular importance on some of the more spectacular gifts—especially the gift of tongues.

1. In order to highlight the priority of love, Paul gives several examples of the extraordinary use of specific spiritual gifts. Make a list the each gift or achievement from these verses, then tell what that gift is without love:

verse 1

✤ What is my extraordinary gift?

✤ What am I if I exercise this gift without love?

verse 2

✤ What are my extraordinary gifts?

✤ What am I if I do them without love?

verse 3

✤ What are my extraordinary gifts/achievements?

✤ What value is there to me if I do them without love?

a. All in all, what do these 3 verses tell you?

2. In 1 Corinthians 3:12-15, Paul tells us something of the same nature. How would the gold, silver, and precious stones be like the *love* in chapter 13?

3. In Revelation 2:2-4, Jesus Christ Himself writes to the church at Ephesus of a problem similar to that of the Corinthians. List the good things they were doing:

✤ verse 2

✤ verse 3

a. With all of these *good deeds* on record, what does Jesus say in verse 4?

b. What is His exhortation to remedy this situation? v. 5

c. What will happen if they don't repent?

"He who has an ear, let him hear what the Spirit says to the churches" Revelation 2:7a

Making It Personal

4. As much as we talk about the importance of the gifts, the priority, Paul says, is *love*. It may be a very good time to consider why you do what you do, as you seek to serve the body of Christ.

✣ Do you use your gifts out of duty?
✣ Do you serve to earn something from God?
✣ Do you serve to feel that you are significant?
or...
✣ Do you serve the body out of love for God and for others?

Digging Deeper

✣ Do your best to summarize today's passage in a couple of sentences.

Memory Verse

"God is love, and the one who abides in love abides in God, and God abides in him." 1 John 4:16b

Day 2
Read 1 Corinthians 13:4-7

I Corinthians 1:7 makes the statement that the Corinthians weren't "lacking in any gift." In other words, they were a very gifted church! But in chapter 8, Paul had to exhort them to concentrate on *love*: "... we know that we all have knowledge. Knowledge makes arrogant, but love edifies." It is the more excellent way! In verses 4-7, Paul takes a snapshot of *love*—and gives us a photograph of *Jesus*.

1. From these verses, make a list of the 14 characteristics of love.

a. What might you say about love, in general, from these verses?

2. What basic truth does 1 John 4:8b and 16b teach us?

    a. How does 1 John 4:9-10 reveal the great way this love has been exemplified to us?

    b. How does John 3:16 put this?

3. In 1 Corinthians 10:31, Paul gave us our motive for everything we do as a Christian—what does it say?

    a. Matthew 22:37-39 gives us the greatest commandments of the law. In a nutshell, what are they?

    b. Considering the way God has loved us, how does it glorify God when we love others above ourselves?

Making It Personal

4. Galatians 5:22-23 lists the fruit of the Spirit of God. If we were trees, these are the kinds of things we could expect to see growing on us! The first fruit mentioned is love! In fact, these assets of the Christian are really personifications of love! Make a list of the fruit of the Spirit.

    a. How is the fruit obtained? (See if you can come up with your own Scriptures for this.)

    b. Is there any fruit that is not evident in your life? From the way you answered the last question, what should you do?

Digging Deeper

✤ Do your best to summarize today's passage in a couple of sentences.

LESSON 16

Day 3
Read 1 Corinthians 13:8-13

What a foundation Paul has laid in these verses so far! When we consider verses 1-7, in light of his teaching on the gifts of the Spirit, we realize that expressing God's love should be the ultimate purpose of every gift! It *is* the more excellent way! Paul begins his thoughts in verse 8 with the words, *love never fails.*

1.   What will fail, according to verse 8?

It's possible that the 3 gifts Paul mentions here were the *cherished* gifts of the Corinthians. Paul names only three gifts, but all the gifts would be included.

   a.   Why will these gifts eventually be done away with? vv. 9-10

   b.   See if you can explain what this means.

Paul uses two illustrations to describe the process of the *partial* being overtaken by the *perfect*: That of a child growing into a man, and that of a mirror which only dimly reflects the reality of the one who looks into it.

2.   What changes when a child becomes a man? Apply this to the gifts.

Obviously the Holy Spirit knows all—John 16:13:14 tells us that He will take of the things of Jesus and share them with us. But God's ways are still a mystery to us. His ways are higher, they are infinite, and we only receive what He chooses to give. The secret things belong to God! But when Jesus comes again, we will see Him face to face!

   a.   What will we know then? v. 12b

   b.   What will be our experience when Jesus is revealed to us? 1 John 3:2b

134

Making It Personal

1 Corinthians 13:12 (NASB) tells us that we are fully known! God knows you intimately! You see dimly—He sees perfectly! He sees your strengths, He knows your weaknesses; but, believe it or not, 1 John 3:2 tells us that when He appears we will be *just like Him*, because we shall see Him just as He is! 1 John 3:3 says, "And everyone who has this hope fixed on Him purifies himself, just as He is pure." Is there any impurity you would like to shed right now, this very day, as you consider the fact that you will one day be *like Him*?

Digging Deeper

✣ Tie this week's memory verse (1 John 4:16b) with the heart of what Paul is saying in this chapter as a whole.

Day 4

Overview of 1 Corinthians 13

Today we will be looking at the passage we have studied this week as a whole. The goal is to find the main lessons the Lord has for us from this chapter. Don't worry about being clever or profound—just do your best!

Find the Facts …

1. See if you can state the <u>content</u> of this week's passage in a couple of sentences. You can use your daily summary statements to help you come up with one main theme or summary of the chapter. (Who is speaking, what is taking place, what is the main subject?)

Look for the Heart …

2. What do you think is the main <u>lesson</u> of this chapter? (What spiritual truths are taught here? Look for a command, a word of exhortation, a promise, etc.)

Hear Him Speak ...

3. Look for a <u>personal application</u> from the content of this chapter. It should come from the lesson you got from the chapter (question 2). How will you apply the lesson to yourself?

4. Was there a particular verse that ministered to you this week? What was it and how did it minister to you?

5. Write out your memory verse *from memory*!

NOTES

.

FIRST CORINTHIANS: *THE WISDOM OF GOD*
LESSON 17
1 CORINTHIANS 14:1-19

⚜

In the midst of Paul's instruction to the Corinthians on the gifts of the Spirit, he wrote an entire chapter on *love*. He entered into that chapter with the words, "But earnestly desire the greater gifts. And I show you a still more excellent way" (1 Corinthians 12:31). He followed the teaching of the chapter devoted to love with these words, which begin our study today: "Pursue love, yet desire earnestly spiritual gifts ..." Love and a desire for the gifts of the Spirit—in particular the gifts that most edify the body—are the key thoughts on the heart of Paul.

Day 1
Read 1 Corinthians 14:1-5

In today's passage, Paul begins to make a distinction in the importance of the gifts as they pertain to the edification of the body of Christ.

1. What does Paul encourage the Corinthians to *pursue*?

   a. Look up the word *pursue* in your dictionary for the general meaning, and then share just how Paul wants us to approach *love*.

2. What are they to *earnestly desire*?

   a. Look up the word *desire* for its general meaning and then share just how Paul wants us to approach *spiritual gifts*.

3. In 1 Corinthians 12:31, Paul said, "Earnestly desire the greater gifts." What does he see as the greater gift here in 14:1?

   a. In verses 2-5, Paul sets out to show why prophecy is the greater gift. What does he say in these verses about:

   ✣ tongues—v. 2?

   ✣ prophecy—v.3?

   ✣ tongues—v. 4a?

   ✣ prophecy—v. 4b?

   ✣ prophecy—v. 5?

   b. From these verses, explain in your own words why prophecy is the greater gift.

The Holman New Testament Commentary on I and II Corinthians says, "The believer who seeks both love and gifts will be especially desirous of the gift of prophecy. The guiding principle … is that the pursuit of spiritual gifts must be joined with a pursuit of love for others."

Making It Personal
4. Are you seeking both love *and* gifts? How should you be approaching love? Are you doing this?

   a. How should you be approaching the gifts? Are you doing this?

   b. Which is the priority?

Digging Deeper

✤ From the study today, see if you can explain the connection between the superiority of prophecy and love.

✤ Do your best to summarize today's passage in a couple of sentences.

Memory Verse

"A new commandment I give to you, that you love one another, even as I have loved you, that you also love one another." John 13:34

Day 2
Read 1 Corinthians 14:6-12

1. In contrast to speaking to the church in tongues, what kind of messages does Paul say will be profitable to them?

   a. Why would these be more profitable than a message in tongues?

2. Paul gives two examples to make his point here—consider each example and share what they convey in your own words:

   verse 7

   verse 8

3. What is the problem with tongues?

   verse 9

   verses 10-11

4. Why is it that Paul needs to make this strong emphasis to the Corinthian church?

    a. The Corinthians were zealous for the gifts—but not necessarily for the right reasons. Why should they seek to excel in the gifts, according to verse 12?

Making It Personal

✤ Do you remember what it means to *edify*? (Look it up if you don't remember.)

✤ Do you remember what it is that *edifies,* according to Paul? (You may see 1 Corinthians 8:1b.)

✤ Apply these thoughts to Paul's statement in verse 12.

✤ Are you doing this?

Digging Deeper

✤ Why might it be said that tongues (in comparison with prophecy) is a *self-edifying* gift?

✤ Why might it be said that prophecy is a *loving* or *giving* gift?

✤ Do your best to summarize today's passage in a couple of sentences.

Day 3
Read 1 Corinthians 14:13-19

1. Because of everything he has already said, what does Paul give as the rule for tongues? v. 13

   a. He gives a couple of more rules for the use of tongues later in this chapter. What further information do these verses give:

      verse 27?

      verse 28?

2. In verse 28, Paul says of the one who speaks in a tongue, "... let him speak to himself and to God." Verse 2 gives a similar description of the one who speaks in a tongue—what description does it give?

   a. In verse 14, Paul describes what happens when a person prays in a tongue. What does it say?

   b. When considering these facts, what is Paul's personal conclusion? v. 15

   c. Why is it important to Paul to *pray with the mind also*? vv. 16-17

3. What personal information does Paul give in verse 18?

   a. While taking this into consideration, what is his preference for the church? v. 19

   b. Why, again, is Paul so strong about his point here?

Making It Personal

✤ From the content of our passage, do you have a new appreciation for the gift of tongues? Share what you have learned about *tongues*.

✤ From the content of our passage, do you have a new appreciation for the gift of prophecy? Share what you have learned about *prophecy*.

Digging Deeper

✤ Tie this week's memory verse (John 13:34) with the heart of what Paul is saying in this chapter as a whole.

Day 4
Overview of 1 Corinthians 14:1-19

Today we will be looking at the passage we have studied this week as a whole. The goal is to find the main lessons the Lord has for us from this chapter. Don't worry about being clever or profound—just do your best!

Find the Facts …

1. See if you can state the <u>content</u> of this week's passage in a couple of sentences. You can use your daily summary statements to help you come up with one main theme or summary of the chapter. (Who is speaking, what is taking place, what is the main subject?)

Look for the Heart …

2. What do you think is the main <u>lesson</u> of this chapter? (What spiritual truths are taught here? Look for a command, a word of exhortation, a promise, etc.)

Hear Him Speak ...

3. Look for a <u>personal application</u> from the content of this chapter. It should come from the lesson you got from the chapter (question 2). How will you apply the lesson to yourself?

4. Was there a particular verse that ministered to you this week? What was it and how did it minister to you?

5. Write out your memory verse *from memory*!

NOTES

FIRST CORINTHIANS: *THE WISDOM OF GOD*
LESSON 18
1 CORINTHIANS 14:20-40
✢

In this portion of chapter 14, Paul continues his teaching on the distinction between tongues and prophecy. He ended our passage last week with very strong words! He said that although he, himself, spoke in tongues, *in the church* he would rather speak *five* words with his understanding, in order that he could teach others, than *10,000* words in a tongue. What might those *five* words have been? Perhaps, *"Jesus died for your sins."*

Day 1
Read 1 Corinthians 14:20-25

As we begin our study today, we need to remember the fact that the Corinthians were putting undo emphasis on the seemingly spectacular gift of tongues. The rest of chapter 14 is really a word of instruction to the church concerning the two gifts we have been studying.

1.   Paul begins this section with an exhortation to the Corinthians *not to be children* ...

    a.   When were they to be *babes*?

    b.   When were they to be *mature*?

2.   Paul has already spoken to them about this problem in chapter 3. What did he communicate to them in the following verses of chapter 3:

    verse 1?

    verse 2?

verse 3?

3.   In the past, how did God use foreign or strange speech? 1 Corinthians 14:21

    a.   What was the result of the *other tongues* according to verse 21?

    b.   What was Paul's conclusion in verse 22?

4.   What would be the response of an unbeliever entering into a worship session of only tongues? v. 23

    a.   Have you ever had this experience? Do you know anyone who has? What did you/they think?

    b.   What would be the response and result of an unbeliever entering into a worship session of prophecy? (List the unbeliever's reaction in the stages Paul gives in these verses.) vv. 24-25

        1)
        2)
        3)
        4)

    c.   Explain the difference between these 2 scenarios (tongues and prophecy).

Making It Personal

5.   Paul says, "... in evil be babes, but in your thinking be mature." Is there a way you can be a *babe in evil* in your circumstance right now? Share.

    a.   What are some ways we can be mature in our thinking (in general)?

b. Is there a way you can be *mature in your thinking* in your circumstances right now? Share.

Digging Deeper

✣ Consider how the Corinthians' *childishness* was shown in their preference for tongues.

✣ How could *mature thinking* correct their discrepancy in this area?

✣ Do your best to summarize today's passage in a couple of sentences.

Memory Verse

"Let all things be done properly and in an orderly manner." 1 Corinthians 14:40

Day 2
Read 1 Corinthians 14:26-33

In this chapter, where Paul seeks to give the Corinthians a proper understanding of the gifts of prophecy and tongues, he gives the goal in verse 12 when he says, "... seek to abound for the edification of the church."

The worship session that Paul describes in the passage at hand may be a little different from what we know today. It may have been more like what we experience in a prayer meeting.

1. Make a list of the elements Paul says may be included in the meeting he describes. See if you can follow each element with a description of what that would be.

    1)
    2)
    3)
    4)
    5)

    a. What again is the goal of all that is done in this meeting? v. 26

Paul now begins to give *specific guidelines* for the gifts we have been studying …

2.   What are the three guidelines for tongues in verse 27?

   1)

   2)

   3)

   a.   One more guideline is given in verse 28. Paul says that if there is no interpreter, the one who speaks in tongues should be *silent*:

   ✤ *Where?* What does this mean?

   ✤ *What should he do instead of speaking in tongues out loud in the church?* What does this mean?

Notice that Paul's *prescription* for this particular situation fits in exactly with his description for the gift of tongues in verse 2.

3.   From verse 29, what is the instruction for prophecy?

   a.   What is the listener's job in this equation?

Warren Wiersbe says it this way: "Each listener must evaluate the message and apply it to his own heart."

4.   What is the guideline for a revelation that comes in the midst of prophecy?

We need to remember that the prophesying referred to here is different from what we know today as preaching. This is not referring to a service in which the Pastor is in the midst of giving his message or reading from Scripture. We might best think of it in terms of a prayer meeting, when each one present is given their opportunity to share in prayer.

a. How should this service proceed according to verse 31?

b. What little bit of information does verse 32 give to the one who has a word or a tongue? Do you know what this means?

c. What is the purpose of the guidelines given here? v. 33 If you see confusion in a worship service, what will that reveal to you?

Making It Personal

5. Speaking of the orderliness of the worship service, Paul says that when the prophets speak, the others are to judge …

a. How should we, as *hearers*, be doing this very thing every time a message proclaimed in our worship services today? (We can let the Bereans be our example in this—see Acts 17:11!) *Do you do this?*

b. How is this in line with Paul's words in verse 20, *"In understanding be mature"*?

Digging Deeper

✠ Do your best to summarize today's passage in a couple of sentences.

Day 3
Read 1 Corinthians 14:34-40

The passage we will look at today can be very confusing and has been very misunderstood. As always, we need to be *mature in our understanding*! We need to compare Scripture with Scripture and also take into consideration the situation of the day.

1. Still in the guideline mode, what guidelines does Paul give for the women in the church in the following verses?

verse 34

verse 35

The word for silent in verse 34 is the same word Paul used in verses 28 and 30—*sigao*—which means to keep silent, keep close (secret, silence), hold peace. In each of these cases (verses 28 and 30), it was given as an assurance of keeping order within the church, which is what our passage today is predominantly about. It has to do with submitting to the *order* of the moment and keeping silent at a particular time. The issue is not men versus women, but confusion versus order.

2.   How does 1 Corinthians 11:5 help us realize that Paul *did* allow women to speak in the church?

Paul's concern has to do with confusion, "For God is not a God of confusion but of peace" (verse 33).

a.   Try to explain what Paul might have been communicating to the men and the women (really husbands and wives) at the Corinthian church about talking during the worship service.

In a word of sarcasm, as well as a word of authority, Paul asks the Corinthians if the word of God had come originally from *them*, or if they were the only church it had reached. Paul himself had brought the teaching of Jesus Christ to the Corinthian church, and he was the one who had the authority to correct them concerning the subject at hand.

3.   What does Paul consider the words he is sharing with them at this time? v. 37

a.   What does he consider anyone who refuses to accept his words as true? v. 38

b.   What is his final word on the subject of prophecy and tongues? v. 39

c.   What is his final word on church etiquette? v. 40

The root word for *properly* (decently, NKJV) means decorously or honestly; the word for *orderly* speaks of arrangement, succession, and dignity.

Making It Personal

4. Is there any way that you, as a woman in the church today, might apply Paul's final word on orderliness to your own church etiquette?

Digging Deeper

✣ Tie this week's memory verse (1 Corinthians 14:40) with the heart of what Paul is saying in this chapter as a whole.

Day 4
Overview of 1 Corinthians 14:20-40

Today we will be looking at the passage we have studied this week as a whole. The goal is to find the main lessons the Lord has for us from this chapter. Don't worry about being clever or profound—just do your best!

Find the Facts ...

1. See if you can state the content of this week's passage in a couple of sentences. You can use your daily summary statements to help you come up with one main theme or summary of the chapter. (Who is speaking, what is taking place, what is the main subject?)

Look for the Heart ...

2. What do you think is the main lesson of this chapter? (What spiritual truths are taught here? Look for a command, a word of exhortation, a promise, etc.)

Hear Him Speak ...

3. Look for a personal application from the content of this chapter. It should come from the lesson you got from the chapter (question 2). How will you apply the lesson to yourself?

4. Was there a particular verse that ministered to you this week? What was it and how did it minister to you?

5. Write out your memory verse *from memory*!

NOTES

FIRST CORINTHIANS: *THE WISDOM OF GOD*
LESSON 19
1 CORINTHIANS 15:1-34

❧

It's interesting when we realize that Paul began his letter to the Corinthians pointing them in the direction of the Cross; he finishes his letter by pointing them in the direction of the Resurrection! Both are central to the message which brings salvation. To reject the concept of resurrection was to reject the very message which had saved them!

Day 1
Read 1 Corinthians 15:1-11

The central message of the Christian faith is the *gospel* or, in other words, *the Good News of Jesus Christ!* Paul begins his words concerning resurrection by *making known to them the gospel.*

Listen to how he says it in The Message:
"Friends, let me go over the Message with you one final time— this Message that I proclaimed and that you made your own; this Message on which you took your stand and by which your life has been saved. (I'm assuming, now, that your belief was the real thing and not a passing fancy, that you're in this for good and holding fast.)" v. 1-2

1. So, Paul had originally preached the gospel message to the Corinthians. What had they done with this message preached by Paul?

   a. What had this message done for them (if, in fact. they were holding fast to it)?

   b. Use verses 3-4 to define the gospel message.

c.   This is the message *by which our life is saved!* How does Romans 10:9 confirm this point?

2.   Verses 5-8 give the *evidence* of Christ's resurrection: He died, He was buried, He rose again, and He was *seen.* Who saw the resurrected Christ?

verse 5

verse 6

verse 7

verse 8

Paul had seen the risen Christ with his own eyes! He had not only seen Him, but Paul received the gospel message from Jesus Himself—"For I delivered to you first of all that which I also received" (v. 3 NKJV).

3.   After stating that Paul had seen Christ last of all, Paul stopped for a moment to consider the ramifications of his last statement. What did he say? v. 9

a.   Do you think Paul was saying here that he wasn't really an apostle? (You may see 2 Corinthians 11:5.) What was he communicating?

.

b.   Was the grace God had shown toward Paul in vain? v. 10

Making It Personal
Paul says, "By the grace of God I am what I am." Paul had been a persecutor of the church. He was now a preacher of the greatest message ever given.

4.   What does it mean to *you* to say, "by the grace of God I am what I am"?

a. Has His grace toward you been in vain? Share your thoughts on this.

Digging Deeper

✤ Notice the repetition of the phrase, *according to the Scriptures*, in verses 3-4. Why is this statement important? Can you think of any Scriptures which foretell the gospel message?

✤ Do your best to summarize today's passage in a couple of sentences.

Memory Verse

"Christ died for our sins, just as the Scriptures said. He was buried, and He was raised from the dead on the third day, as the Scriptures said." 1 Cor. 15:3-4 (NLT)

Day 2
Read 1 Corinthians 15:12-19

In verse 12, we have evidence that some of the Corinthians were, in fact, denying the resurrection of the dead. They weren't necessarily denying *Christ's* resurrection, specifically, but the fact that believers would be raised.

1. Starting in verse 13, Paul begins a series of "if" thoughts. Share from these verses what would be the case *if there were no resurrection from the dead:*

    verse 13

    verse 14

    verse 15

    verse 16

    verse 17

    verse 18

    verse 19

Digging Deeper

✤ According to Paul's thoughts, can you really be a Christian without believing in the Resurrection? (Why would our faith be futile it there was no resurrection of the dead?)

✤ Why would it be true that the Corinthians would still be in their sins if Christ had not been raised?

✤ Considering what you know about the Paul's life and ministry, why do you think it might be that Paul said, "If we have hoped in Christ in this life only, we are of all men most to be pitied."?

✤ Do your best to summarize today's passage in a couple of sentences.

Day 3
Read 1 Corinthians 15:20-34

The NIV translates the beginning of verse 20 in this wonderful way: "But Christ has *indeed* been raised from the dead"! All that Paul shared in the "if" verses (verses 13-19) can be entirely disregarded, because Christ had indeed been raised—Paul had seen Him with his own eyes!

In verses 21-22, using Adam's sin and Christ's sacrifice, Paul paints the picture between death and life. The Life Application Bible Commentary on 1 & 2 Corinthians says, "What we believe about this life and the afterlife depends on what Jesus did with death."

1. What was Adam's part in our death sentence?

   verse 21

   verse 22

a.   What did Christ *do with death*?

   verse 21

   verse 22

2.   Verse 23 gives the order of resurrections.

   ✣ Who is raised first? What is He called?

   ✣ Who is raised next?

3.   In verses 24-28, Paul gives a sort of overview of what will happen next. Share from these verses exactly what will take place.

   verse 24-25

   verse 26

   verse 27-28

Alan Redpath says that these verses—in particular verses 24-25—are the "greatest glimpse into the ultimate future that the Bible gives to us."

In verse 29, Paul comes back again to an "if" question. This time he speaks of the *living* being baptized for the *dead*. His question is, if the dead do not rise (or are not resurrected), why would men be baptized for them? He doesn't say anything about the practice—not condoning or condemning it—just that it is being done and that it makes no sense for them to do this, if they don't believe in resurrection.

Another "if" statement is implied in verse 30. We might begin the verse this way: If Christ is not raised from the dead, why do we stand in jeopardy every hour? In verse 31, Paul speaks of dying daily, and in verse 32 of fighting the wild beasts of Ephesus.

4.   What is Paul communicating in these verses?

a. What is his conclusion? v. 32b

b. Do you understand what Paul is saying here?

5. In verses 33-34, Paul finishes this section with three strong words of exhortation. What are they?

1)

2)

3)

a. From the context of the chapter so far, why do you think Paul is so strong with them here?

Making It Personal

6. Because Christ has indeed been raised, and because **He** is the *first fruit* of those who have fallen asleep (verse 20), what does that imply about us?

There is a saying that goes this way: *Born once, die twice; born twice, die once.*

a. From verse 22:

✝ What happens to those who are only born into Adam?

✝ What happens to those who are born, again, into Christ?

If you are only born into Adam, then your fate is death. If you have been born-again into Christ, then you will live! There is a choice to be made—and *you* must make it! Have you chosen life? (Deut. 30:19)

Digging Deeper

✝ Tie this week's memory verse (1 Corinthians 15:3-4 NLT) with the heart of what Paul is saying in this chapter as a whole.

Day 4
Overview of 1 Corinthians 15:1-34

Today we will be looking at the passage we have studied this week as a whole. The goal is to find the main lessons the Lord has for us from this chapter. Don't worry about being clever or profound—just do your best!

Find the Facts …

1. See if you can state the <u>content</u> of this week's passage in a couple of sentences. You can use your daily summary statements to help you come up with one main theme or summary of the chapter. (Who is speaking, what is taking place, what is the main subject?)

Look for the Heart …

2. What do you think is the main <u>lesson</u> of this chapter? (What spiritual truths are taught here? Look for a command, a word of exhortation, a promise, etc.)

Hear Him Speak …

3. Look for a <u>personal application</u> from the content of this chapter. It should come from the lesson you got from the chapter (question 2). How will you apply the lesson to yourself?

4. Was there a particular verse that ministered to you this week? What was it and how did it minister to you?

5. Write out your memory verse *from memory*!

NOTES

FIRST CORINTHIANS: *THE WISDOM OF GOD*
LESSON 20
1 CORINTHIANS 15:35-58

The subject matter of chapter 15 is resurrection, both the resurrection of Christ and the resurrection of the believer. In last week's portion of the chapter, Paul answered the question of whether or not there actually is a resurrection. He said, *yes, as a matter of fact, there is!* This week he tackles the question of how, exactly, that resurrection will take place. This final section of Paul's letter is truly the high point of the entire letter, as he gives us all—Corinthians and modern-day believers alike—great hope for the future!

Day 1
Read 1 Corinthians 15:35-41

1. What two possible questions, according to Paul, might be raised with regard to the resurrection?

    1)

    2)

    a. Although these might seem somewhat plausible questions, what is Paul's take on the one that might ask them? v. 36

To Paul, there is no question as to whether or not there is a resurrection. Therefore, he is impatient with anyone who doesn't readily grasp the truth. According to what follows, Paul's argument is that nature itself teaches the concept.

To present the truth of resurrection, Paul uses the example of sowing. To help us understand his analogy, we might think of planting a flower.

2. When you wish to have a particular flower in your garden, do you plant the *body* of the flower you want to grow there? Or, does the *seed* you plant look like the flower you are hoping for? What do you plant? v. 37

   a. How does the body come, according to verse 38?

   b. How different is the flower that grows from the seed that was originally sown? (It might help to get a mental picture of this.)

   c. Consider how this analogy explains the resurrection.

3. What are some of the different kinds of *flesh* God has created? v. 39

   a. What 2 kinds of *bodies* are there? v. 40

   b. What different kinds of *glory* are there? vv. 40-41

   c. Is God limited in any way when it comes to creating? How does that thought help us understand His ability to create resurrected bodies?

Making It Personal

We all have things about our natural bodies that we dislike—we're too thin, too heavy, too tall, too short, we need glasses, we can't sing, etc., etc., etc.! But one day our natural bodies will die (unless the Lord comes first!) and 1 Corinthians 15 promises that we will receive new bodies. We will be like that bare seed that was sown so that a beautiful flower might appear in its place.

4. What are some of the things you are looking forward to as you consider what your new body will be like?

a. What truth are we taught in Romans 8:29?

b. What does 1 John 3:2 tell us? What hope does this give you?

Digging Deeper

✣ Speaking of His own death in John 12:24, Jesus sets forth the same truth that Paul is teaching in our verses today. What does He say there? What truth is He teaching about Himself?

✣ Can you apply this truth to yourself?

✣ Do your best to summarize today's passage in a couple of sentences.

Memory Verse
"But thanks be to God, who gives us the victory through our Lord Jesus Christ." 1 Corinthians 15:57

Day 2
Read 1 Corinthians 15:42-49

Paul begins this passage with the words, "So also is the resurrection of the dead." He is obviously referring back to something, so we look back at what we have just read and realize he is still talking about that seed which is sown. Like a seed that is sown and grows into a beautiful plant, so it will be with the resurrection of the dead. One thing is sown, another is raised.

1. Verses 42-44 give us the most exciting and glorious news, as they portray the contrast between what is sown and what is raised, with regard to the human body. Write down what these verses convey, and spend a few moments in your dictionary looking up the words that describe the before and after of resurrection.

The body is sown...   *The body is raised...*

✣ verse 42
    definition:

165

The body is sown...	*The body is raised...*

✤ verse 43a
   definition:

✤ verse 43b
   definition:

   -
✤ verse 44a
   definition:

Paul says in verse 44, "If there is a natural body, there is also a spiritual body." In the following verses, Paul reveals that if something is true of Adam, then *something greater* is true of Christ!

2. From the each of the following verses, state what is true of Adam and the greater thing that is true of Christ:

   ✤ verse 45

      What is true of Adam?

      What greater thing is true of Christ?

   ✤ verse 46

      What came first?

      What greater thing came afterward?

   ✤ verse 47

      What is true of Adam?

      What greater thing is true of Christ?

   ✤ verse 48

      What is true of us in Adam?

      What greater thing is true of us in Christ?

✤ verse 49

What have we borne of Adam?

What greater thing will we bear of Christ?

Digging Deeper
Look up the following verses that give you a glimpse of what your heavenly body will be like:

Jesus resurrected body: Philippians 3:20-21

Immortal and glorious: 1 Corinthians 15:50-54; 2 Corinthians 5:1-4

Perfect: Philippians 1:6; Revelation 21:1-5

Clothed in righteousness: Daniel 12:3; Matthew 13:43

✤ Do your best to summarize today's passage in a couple of sentences.

Day 3
Read 1 Corinthians 15:50-58

1. Paul begins this section with a very strong and important statement: Flesh and blood cannot inherit the kingdom of God.

    a. What does this imply for those of us who hope to go to heaven? And how does this apply to the process of resurrection we have been discussing?

The bottom line is—*we must be changed!* Paul has the privilege of delivering the amazing news of this amazing mystery!

2. What is the amazing mystery? v. 51

    a. How will this happen? v. 52

3. Because flesh and blood cannot inherit the kingdom of God, what must take place for the church to be taken up to heaven? v. 53

    a. What will be the outcome of this supernatural transformation? v. 54

4. Verses 56-57 explain why we can take up the chant, "O death, where is your victory? O death, where is your sting"? (verse 55). From these verses, do your best to explain why we have victory over death.

5. The outcome of Paul's teaching on the resurrection is an exhortation to all believers. Read verse 58 and share the exhortation of Paul.

    a. How does this exhortation tie in and finish his thoughts on resurrection?

Making It Personal

6. Do you know someone who has died in the Lord—maybe a mother, father, husband, or child? Consider verses 42-44, along with our verses today and the contrast of their state at death with their future state of victory. How do these thoughts bless you today?

Digging Deeper

✠ Tie this week's memory verse (1 Corinthians 15:57) with the heart of what Paul is saying in this chapter as a whole.

Day 4
Overview of 1 Corinthians 15:35-58

Today we will be looking at the passage we have studied this week as a whole. The goal is to find the main lessons the Lord has for us from this chapter. Don't worry about being clever or profound—just do your best!

Find the Facts ...

1. See if you can state the <u>content</u> of this week's passage in a couple of sentences. You can use your daily summary statements to help you come up with one main theme or summary of the chapter. (Who is speaking, what is taking place, what is the main subject?)

Look for the Heart ...

2. What do you think is the main <u>lesson</u> of this chapter? (What spiritual truths are taught here? Look for a command, a word of exhortation, a promise, etc.)

Hear Him Speak ...

3. Look for a <u>personal application</u> from the content of this chapter. It should come from the lesson you got from the chapter (question 2). How will you apply the lesson to yourself?

4. Was there a particular verse that ministered to you this week? What was it and how did it minister to you?

5. Write out your memory verse *from memory*!

NOTES

FIRST CORINTHIANS: *THE WISDOM OF GOD*
LESSON 21
1 CORINTHIANS 16

❧

As we come to the end of 1 Corinthians, we enter chapter 16 and feel as if it is almost anti-climactic. We have just left the heights of heaven, as we considered the resurrection of Christ and the future resurrection of every believer. Chapter 16 brings us right back down to earth with the taking up of a collection! Alan Redpath says, "A Christian is a man whose heart is in heaven but whose feet are on the ground." He also gives his own wonderful perspective on chapter 16 as he says, "This chapter is the crown of all the teaching of the Corinthian letter." We can sum up Paul's teaching to the Corinthians in this letter with these words, "You shall love the Lord your God with all your heart, and with all your soul, and with all your mind … You shall love your neighbor as yourself" (Matthew 22:37, 39).

Day 1
Read 1 Corinthians 16:1-4

With the words, "Now concerning," we are brought back to another topic that the Corinthians had addressed with Paul. Their question wasn't whether or not they were to take up a collection, it seems this had already been addressed at a previous time. This question seems to have dealt with the *way* in which the collection was to be taken.

1. For whom was the collection to be taken? v. 1

   a. How does Romans 15:25-26 further designate who these people were?

   b. Romans 15:27 goes on to explain *why* Paul felt it was important for the Corinthians to take up this collection. Why was this?

2. In Romans 15:26, we're given two areas involved in sending aid to the saints in Jerusalem. Who were they?

    a. As Paul begins to give instructions for taking up the collection, whom does he use as his example in directing them? 1 Corinthians 16:1

    b. What do you learn about Paul and his heart as you consider what we have looked at so far?

3. Verse 2 is very clear in the NLT: "On every Lord's Day, each of you should put aside some amount of money in relation to what you have earned and save it for this offering. Don't wait until I get there and then try to collect it all at once." Using this translation, answer the following questions:

    ✤ When were they to put this money aside? How does that apply to us today?

    ✤ In three words, who was to give?

    ✤ How were they to know what to give?

    ✤ Why do you think Paul didn't want them to wait until he came to collect the money?

    ✤ Why might Paul have wanted *them* to choose who would take the money to Jerusalem? v. 3-4

Making It Personal

4. Paul's instructions to Corinth are perfect for us to follow in our giving to the church today. Is there anything you learned in these verses that will change how you give?

5. 2 Corinthians 9:7-8 give the *heart* perspective of the giver. From these verses, share:

    ✤ *How a person is to give.* v. 7

✤ *Why a person is able to give.* v. 8

a. Have you had the right perspective in giving? Share your thoughts.

Digging Deeper
✤ Do your best to summarize today's passage in a couple of sentences.

Memory Verse
"He who testifies to these things says, 'Surely I am coming quickly.' Amen. Even so, come, Lord Jesus!" Revelation 22:20 NKJV

Day 2
Read 1 Corinthians 16:5-9

We remember that Paul is on his third missionary journey. It is now near the end of his three-year stay in Ephesus and only a few short years before he would be imprisoned in Jerusalem (ironically at the time and occasion of delivering the collection he had been taking up from the churches—Acts 21:15; 24:17). In the next verses, we will see what his tentative plans were at this time.

1. From these verses, describe Paul's intentions for visiting the Corinthians:

   verse 5

   verse 6

   verse 7

   a. You may wish to look at a map of Paul's third missionary journey and see the path he did eventually take as he left Ephesus: he went through the area of Macedonia to Corinth and then back again through Macedonia and on to Jerusalem.

2. What was his immediate plan, according to verse 8?

a. See if you can remember what time of year Pentecost would be celebrated. From that thought, you can get an idea of the time period Paul planned on traveling through Macedonia to get to Corinth to spend the winter.

b. Why was it Paul's plan to stay in Ephesus until Pentecost? v. 9a

3. What had been the case regarding Paul's ministry to Ephesus, when he wanted to go there on his second missionary journey—was there an open door for him at that time? See Acts 16:6

a. Consider why Ephesus might have been shut off to Paul before this time. (You might think about the people in Ephesus, as well as Paul, himself.)

b. With the open door came—what? 1 Corinthians 16:9b

c. Would this have been a surprise?

We notice Paul's obvious reaction was to continue on in spite of the adversaries. His plan was to stay put!

Making It Personal

4. Have you experienced a time that a door for service was closed to you? (Maybe you are in such a time right now.) How did you react, and what did you do, when you realized the door was closed?

a. What does Jesus say about *doors* in Revelation 3:7?

b. Is there a wide door of effective service open to you just now? Are there many adversaries? How are you responding to this open door? How does Revelation 3:8 encourage you as you approach your *open door*?

Digging Deeper
✤ Do your best to summarize today's passage in a couple of sentences.

Day 3
Read 1 Corinthians 16:10-24

As we studied the first half of this chapter, we were given the worldwide perspective of Paul, as many areas were brought into the picture—Galatia, Jerusalem, Macedonia, Achaia, and Ephesus. In the rest of the passage, which we will study today, *people* will be brought into the picture—as many of those who were ministering with Paul will be mentioned by name. Alan Redpath says that in this chapter *the whole church comes into view!*

1. Let's look at each of those mentioned by name in this chapter, and what Paul has to say about them.

   Timothy—v. 10-11
   ✤ What do you already know about Timothy?

   ✤ What does Paul say about him here?

   Apollos—v. 12
   ✤ What do you already know about Apollos?

   ✤ What does Paul say about him here?

   The household of Stephanas—v. 15-16
   ✤ What does Paul say about them here?

   Stephanas, Fortunatus, and Achaicus—v. 17-18
   ✤ What does Paul say about them here?

2. From verses 19-20, who sends their greetings to the Corinthians?

    a. Look briefly at Revelation 1:4 and chapters 2-3 to see to whom the words, *the churches of Asia* may refer. (There were many churches started by Paul in the province of Asia.) List these here.

    b. Share what you remember about Aquila and Priscilla.

    c. Although Paul had probably dictated the majority of this letter to the Corinthians, how did he ensure to them that he was personally involved in the writing? v.21

3. Paul gives two final words of exhortation to the Corinthians as he finishes his letter to them. The first word is found in verses 13-14 and has 5 parts. List them here:

1)
2)
3)
4)
5)

Paul's final thoughts are strong—as they should be! Think of the final words you would say to your children, as you went out the door and left them for a while. Might they be like these?

    a. The second word is actually a warning. What is it? v. 22

Paul finishes his letter with three words ... The word, *Maranatha,* which means, O Lord, come! With a prayer for grace, (even as he had begun the letter with this same prayer—see 1 Corinthians 1:3)—and with a final mention of his love for them, "My love be with you all in Christ Jesus. Amen."

Making It Personal
As Paul considered the curse that would rest on any who didn't love Jesus, he finished with the word, Maranatha—O Lord, come*!*

4. What is your heart on the soon coming of our Lord? Do you want him to come quickly? Share your thoughts on this.

a. What are you doing to be ready? For inspiration and motivation, read the parable of the 10 virgins in Matthew 25:1-13.

b. How are you occupying while you wait?

"Look, He is coming with the clouds,
and every eye will see Him ... So shall it be! Amen."
Revelation 1:7 NIV

Digging Deeper

✤ See if you can summarize, in a few sentences, the entire letter Paul has written to the Corinthians!

Day 4
Overview of 1 Corinthians 16

Today we will be looking at the passage we have studied this week as a whole. The goal is to find the main lessons the Lord has for us from this chapter. Don't worry about being clever or profound—just do your best!

Find the Facts ...

1. See if you can state the content of this week's passage in a couple of sentences. You can use your daily summary statements to help you come up with one main theme or summary of the chapter. (Who is speaking, what is taking place, what is the main subject?)

Look for the Heart ...

2. What do you think is the main lesson of this chapter? (What spiritual truths are taught here? Look for a command, a word of exhortation, a promise, etc.)

Hear Him Speak ...

3. Look for a <u>personal application</u> from the content of this chapter. It should come from the lesson you got from the chapter (question 2). How will you apply the lesson to yourself?

4. Was there a particular verse that ministered to you this week? What was it and how did it minister to you?

5. Write out your memory verse *from memory*!

NOTES

ABOUT THE AUTHOR

Linda has dedicated her life to serving the Lord as a teacher, writer, and speaker. While teaching the Word of God, training leaders, and speaking at retreats and other women's ministry functions, she has also written curriculum for over 20 books of the Bible.

If you would be interested in having more information about her ministry or purchase her books/Bible Studies, please visit her blog at www.lindaosborne.net, or email her at myutmost1@aol.com.

Made in the USA
Las Vegas, NV
05 January 2022

40423325R00103